D0009183

So You Think You're Not Religious?

For Sara,

Jim Adams
2/5/89

So You Think You're Not Religious?

* * *

A Thinking Person's Guide To The Church

James R. Adams

1989

Cowley Publications
Cambridge, Massachusetts

Copyright © 1989 by James R. Adams

Published in the United States of America by Cowley
Publications, a division of the Society of St. John the
Evangelist. All rights reserved. No portion of this book may
be reproduced in whole or in part without the consent of
Cowley Publications except in the case of brief quotations
embodied in critical articles and reviews.

International Standard Book Number: 0-936384-69-7
Library of Congress Number: 88-37625

Cover Design by Daniel Earl Thaxton

Library of Congress Cataloging-in-Publications Data
Adams, James R., 1934–
    So you think you're not religious?: a thinking person's guide
to the church / James R. Adams.
        p. cm.
    ISBN 0-936384-69-7 : $8.95
    1. Apologetics—20th century. 2. Episcopal Church—
Doctrines. 3. Anglican Communion—Doctrines. I. Title.
BT1102.A34 1989
239—dc 19   88-37625

Cowley Publications
980 Memorial Drive
Cambridge, MA 02138

To
Ginny
my favorite skeptic

Celebrating James R. Adams'
So You Think You're Not Religious?

"If you are someone who recoils at churchy gibberish, uses the Bible as a bookend, gags at the sanctimonious, squirms during the Creed—in other words thinks darkening the door of a church is a waste of time—*read this book.*"

—Amory Houghton, Jr.
U.S. House of Representatives

"As refreshingly honest a book as I have read in a long while. A good book for the health of the Church and for the soul's health of many a Christian who has been unwilling or unable to talk about his or her difficulty with the so-called 'faith once delivered.'"

—Paul M. van Buren

"Jim Adams has written a moving testament to the relevance of the faith for those to whom the traditional formulations no longer speak."

—Verna Dozier

"Addresses all who hope for a way to love God by loving life in the world."

—The Rt Revd Bennett J. Sims
The Institute for Servant Leadership

"Jim Adams has discovered helpful wisdom for both discouraged pastors and independent thinkers. Written in accessible language, out of a wealth of pastoral experience, this book shows how the Christian tradition speaks to the deepest concerns of those for whom believing isn't *easy.*"

—Celia Allison Hahn
The Alban Institute

"Clergy and laity concerned with the communication of the Gospel in a secular society will be absorbed and stimulated by James Adams' work."

—John C. Harris
author of *Power, Stress and Ministry*

Table of Contents

Chapter 7
THE BIRTH OF A CHILD—Holy Baptism

Chapter 8
THE BURIAL OF THE DEAD

Chapter 9
SUNDAY—Other Rituals for Other Transitions

Appendix

PREFACE

When I was new to the Episcopal Church, I asked one of the clergy how I could find out what Episcopalians believe. He said, "Catch one and ask."

I caught a few, asked, and kept getting contradictory replies. The longer I stayed in the Episcopal Church, the more curious I became about why Episcopalians have so many and varied beliefs and ways of doing things. So it was with some eagerness in 1979, while on my second sabbatical leave from St. Mark's Church on Capitol Hill in Washington, that I began a serious study of the origins of Christianity in Britain. Because the Episcopal Church in the United States traces its roots to the church in England, I thought that living and studying there would give me a better understanding of the contradictions found in what is generally called "the Anglican tradition". I was not disappointed.

Christianity in Britain developed along somewhat different lines from anywhere else in the world. At least by the fourth century the church was well established among the Celtic people who inhabited this island on the extreme edge of the Roman Empire. When the Roman legions withdrew in the year 410, the Celtic people were left to defend themselves against the onslaught of the Angles, Saxons, Jutes, and Frisians—the people who collectively came to be known as the "English". The Celtic Christians who survived the invasion retreated to the remote regions of Wales and Cornwall. For a century and a half they carried on their religion with little influence from Rome or Western Europe. Left on their own, the Celtic Christians developed a church dedicated to a simple way of life marked by contemplative prayer, high moral standards of behavior, and individual openness to the presence of God. During this same period, the church in the rest of Europe saw itself as the inheritor of the structure, traditions, and splendor of imperial Rome. Representatives from these two quite different Christian traditions eventually established missions among the English. Although the better-organized Roman Christians soon became the dominant force, Celtic Christianity persisted as a strong influence. The church in England as a result of this blending of opposite values was filled with contradictions from the beginning. To complicate matters further, Christians in England never really gave up many of the pagan customs that had been practiced on the island since ancient times. Episcopalians frequently contradict each other because the Episcopal Church offers such a rich tradition—a blend of Celtic and Roman Christianity with pagan British and English customs.

This blend is a definite advantage to skeptical people with an interest in a religious community. They can pick and choose among the diverse elements that make up the Anglican tradition to work out a meaningful pattern for themselves. They can also find meaning in the sense of continuity with the past that such an ancient tradition makes possible.

Convinced that the Anglican tradition has much to offer skeptics, I was delighted to run across an article in the *London Sunday Times* entitled "The Ideal Home for Agnostics", which turns out be be a quote from T. S. Eliot describing to the Church of England. The author of the article notes George Orwell's observation that the English were indifferent to serious religious belief but retained "a deep tinge of Christian feeling". After stating that Orwell used imprecise words because he was describing an imprecise thing, the article poses a rhetorical question: "and in the grandeur of creation what thing has been more splendidly imprecise than the Church of England?"

Wanting to help Episcopalians appreciate our splendid imprecision and wanting to show skeptics that they can find a home in the Anglican tradition, I decided to spend my third sabbatical writing this book. I am deeply grateful to the vestry and congregation of St. Mark's for giving me this time away from my usual responsibilities and for providing me with a computer to facilitate my writing.

By supporting me in this venture, the people of St. Mark's were acting in characteristic fashion. For the past twenty-two years we have worked together in developing the kind of parish life that helps equip people to function effectively in their daily lives. The principles that have shaped this effort came to us through the educational theory and discipline of Charles F. Penniman, the founder of the Educational Center in St. Louis. Dr. Penniman's approach to theology helped us discover how Christianity could be more than an ideology and an organization. The church can be an arena where people discover the resources they need when they find their lives under pressure.

In particular I appreciate the time and effort expended by the five people from the congregation who advised me all through the project: David Meade, Crane Miller, Jim Kelley, Peter Powers, and Celia Hahn, and by my associate Susan Gresinger. Verna Dozier and Janice Gregory also offered many helpful suggestions.

The two people who were probably the most indispensible throughout the process were the secretaries at St. Mark's, Betty Smith and Mildred Wheat, who printed out the countless revisions, corrected them, and made copies for all the readers. I cannot thank them enough for all of their help.

As I reached the final stages of producing an acceptable manuscript, I came to be increasingly grateful for the encouragement and sound advice of Cynthia Shattuck of Cowley Publications. The only person on whom I relied more heavily was my wife Ginny, whose healthy skepticism has sustained me over the years; she read and corrected the final version.

In becoming acquainted with the Anglican tradition with the aid of this book, the reader will need to have a copy of The Book of Common Prayer (1979). A contemporary English translation of the Bible would also be useful in working with the material in several of the chapters. Either the Revised Standard Version or the New English Bible would be best. Most of the biblical quotations come from one of these two sources.

James R. Adams
Washington, DC
August 10, 1988

Part One

***

Skepticism
and Belief

"You know, that Sunday I came to a service was the first time I had been in church, except for weddings, in at least ten years." He was clearly ill at ease, although he seemed to have relaxed a little when I accepted the beer he offered. "I'm afraid you may be wasting your time," he went on, almost apologetically, "because, you see, I could never believe all those things you have to believe to be a Christian. I was brought up in the church, went to Sunday School, and a youth group when I was in junior high, but I stopped going when I started high school and never went back. We had a lot of bull sessions about religion when I was in college. For a while I called myself an atheist. Now I guess I'd say that agnostic fits me better. It's not that I'm sure that God doesn't exist; it's just that I can't believe all those things you are supposed to believe."

When I asked him what sorts of things he had in mind, he shrugged and replied, "Oh, you know, the virgin birth, Jesus rising from the dead, Jonah in the whale, that sort of thing." When I told him that we had something in common because I could not believe that those things were historical events, he looked startled, and blurted out, "But you're a priest! I thought you had to believe that stuff to get ordained." I assured him that I had tried hard but had failed to become a believer, but that I had found a great deal of value in the church that might interest him, too.

I have run into many people like me and like that young man, who cannot believe all those things Christians are supposed to believe but still find themselves drawn to the church. Over the years I have found ways of practicing Christianity in the Episcopal Church that have been deeply satisfying to me and to people in the congregation I serve; I think they might be useful to other skeptics as well. It is a tragedy that many honest skeptics do not realize that they can find resources in the church to help them live more meaningful and effective lives without having to sacrifice their intellectual integrity. This book offers advice on how to be a practicing Christian without becoming a believer.

The terms "skeptic" and "believer" are more than a little imprecise when used in ordinary conversation. What I mean by "believer" is a person who accepts a body of opinion or a system of propositions without regard for empirical evidence. For me a "true believer" is one who holds to these opinions or propositions even in the face of contrary evidence, judging all those who hold opposing opinions to be in error. A "skeptic" is quite a different sort of person, being one who instinctively doubts, questions, or disagrees with assertions presented without verifiable evidence. A skeptic is simply unable to accept religious dogma.

Many practicing Episcopalians also harbor serious intellectual reservations about some of the things they say and hear in church, and know very little about their Anglican heritage. Although this book will not tell them the whole story, it will give them one way of dealing with their semi-skepticism and one way of looking at the traditions and rituals of their church.

My hope in preparing this book has also been that clergy and lay leaders in the Episcopal Church will take more of an interest in a ministry among skeptics. Trying to make believers out of them may not always be the most effective and the most loving approach. I am convinced that our cities are full of people who could profit from an association with the Episcopal church and that the church has a responsibility to offer these people the resources of our heritage without placing them in the untenable position of choosing between their integrity and the practice of Christianity.

Chapter 1
WHAT THE CHURCH CAN OFFER SKEPTICS

Skeptical people cannot accept the assumptions of any religious groups that are not consistent with what they know of science and of history. A skeptic might be attracted to the teachings of Jesus of Nazareth but would have difficulty believing that Jesus was born of a woman who had never had sexual intercourse, was able to walk on water, and was raised from the dead. As a rule they place a higher value on their intellectual integrity than they do on being approved by other people. Religious conformity may not be an option for skeptics because they are compelled to ask questions and to challenge ideas that do not make sense to them. They do not want to be affiliated with groups whose principles they cannot honestly support.

Many educated, intelligent skeptics harbor a guilty secret, however. They envy believers. They would not want to be identified as religious people, especially Christians. Christians, skeptics have discovered, are not an especially attractive lot. Still, believers at times seem to have advantages that make them secretly the envy of non-believers.

Community
Believers have a community. They have people who know them by name, who look in on them when they are sick, who celebrate their triumphs with them, who see them through their grief when someone dies, who care about them as individuals.

People who live in small towns or in the ethnic neighborhoods of large cities may have a sense of community, but for most people urban areas can be lonely places. You meet people at the office, and you can join a little theater group, and you can try to keep up with your old college friends, but basically, you know that you are alone. You can try to cope with your loneliness by hanging out at a bar or watching a lot of television, but you may still feel isolated.

Loneliness is not limited to single people. A husband and wife may have each other, but living in a vast urban area they may find it difficult to feel connected to anyone outside of their own household. The sense of isolation may even increase if they have children. Parents can become acutely aware that they do not have the support system enjoyed by previous generations when grandparents and maiden aunts were generally available to help. The responsibility for children can be frightening without a community to help with their nurture and training. Parents need more support and direction than a PTA, a teacher, or even a school guidance counselor can provide.

Christians have always had a strong interest in community. The New Testament shows a concern for community that is not always apparent because the Greek word for community, *koinonia*, appears in such a variety of forms. It can be translated not only as community but also as association, fellowship, partnership, participation, or close relationship. The root of the word is a verb, which means to share; that is, to divide responsibility between two people or among members of a larger group. Early Christians placed a high value on community because for the most part they were urban people who had been uprooted from their native villages. In the first century, Christianity was primarily an urban phenomenon. Urbanization produced a sense of dislocation in people who left an age-old tribal culture for life in the cities. The church drew most of its first Gentile members from this dislocated population.

Twentieth century America has much in common with the world in which Christianity first flourished: rapid communication and transportation, urbanization, and social dislocation. The people who have migrated to our cities from small towns and rural areas have had difficulty in replacing the kind of communal ties that once held their lives together. A person with no religious convictions whatsoever may be drawn to a church because of a desire to be part of a community.

Ritual
The rites of passage provided by the church may also look attractive to skeptical people. If you do not have the ritual

forms of a community to see you though transitions, how do you celebrate the birth of a child? how do you get married? how do you provide for a funeral? Birth, marriage, and death trigger powerful emotions that need healthy expression. People who do not have access to the ritual forms of a worshiping community are much more likely to have a difficult time recovering from grief than those who maintain a church connection. They have no accepted way of expressing their feelings of loss and sorrow so these feelings are turned inward, a process that frequently leads to depression. Without an accepted ritual, grieving people are also deprived of the means by which friends and relatives could express their concern. Genuine sympathy and affection can seldom be put into words and appropriate occasions for receiving support may be difficult to find, so people without a religious community often find themselves alone with their grief, a situation that may deepen their depression and impede their recovery.

Besides the major passages of a personal nature, most people seem to need ritual forms to mark the routine rhythms of life. The days all blend into monotonous repetition if one day on the calendar looks like every other day. One week is like any other without special days or events. The seasons come and go in a city almost without notice unless you find some way to mark the changes. For centuries the church gave shape to the passage of time by introducing the seven-day week of the Jews to the Gentile world, by establishing holy days for special observances, and by giving theological significance to the changing seasons.

As the church lost its dominant position in Western society, the central meaning of these ritual forms and festivals disappeared. To make up for the missing holy days and observances, our secular society has set aside what we persist in calling "holidays" although few recall that special days once had something to do with holiness. Most of these modern holidays celebrate relatively recent events—such as the armistice that ended World War I—or honor people—like Martin Luther King, Jr., who made a major contribution to the country. Taken as an annual cycle of observances, they leave many people unsatisfied.

Although many Americans with no church connections observe the Christian celebrations of Christmas and Easter, the religious significance of these holidays has become so well camouflaged that their purpose is now obscure. As a result, many skeptical people are left with no workable system for marking transitions and giving meaning to the passage of time.

Ethics

The secularization of society may also have produced a crisis in ethics. According to a fair number of secular observers, the last quarter of the twentieth century has been a time of moral decay in America. Columnists in newspapers and magazines lament the decline of ethical standards both in public and private life. They suggest that doctors and lawyers as well as politicians and business people are motivated primarily by greed with little concern for the welfare of society. These social critics have concluded that young people quite naturally incorporate the prevailing morality into their way of life, with juvenile delinquency and teen-age pregnancy the obvious symptoms of a culture that has lost its moral bearings. The ethical level of the present generation may actually not be much different from that of previous ages, but many skeptical people yearn for higher standards of morality in society.

Intelligent people once thought they could produce an ethical outlook on life without having to put up with the absurdities of religion. That seemed like a reasonable possibility, but morality unhooked from religion appears to lack vitality.

Skeptical people may know that the church is a corrupt institution and they may not be favorably impressed by the behavior of church leaders, but they may also see that church people should know better. Believers simply fail to live up to the best they know. Because they profess higher ethical standards than those they employ in determining their behavior, Christians sometimes pass on their ideals to the next generation in spite of themselves. Much of the positive response to the black people who demanded an end to racial segregation in the South came from young, white people who took seriously what they were taught in Sunday school. They could not reconcile white oppression of black people with the concept of loving your neighbor as yourself.

Skeptical people may also see that if they take morality seriously, then religion may become a necessity. Religion may have arisen because ancient people were confronted by moral contradictions. For example, human beings seem to share with many other animals an instinct for kin altruism. Like the ruffed grouse who feigns injury to lead predators away from her nest, primitive human beings would risk their lives to protect the lives of their children. At some point in their evolution, however, people realized that the long-term well-being of their kin depended on the well-being of society as a whole. Today we generally accept both ethical principles: it is a good thing to protect one's family, and it is a good thing to promote the general welfare of all people.

So what is the morally proper response when your child needs a liver transplant and you know that the hospitals do not have enough donated organs to meet the demand? Do you do everything in your political and financial power to get your child the operation he needs to survive, or do you work for the fair and equitable distribution of the scarce donor organs? It is in such ethical dilemmas that even skeptics may ask the basic religious question, "What does this all mean?" Skeptics know that the church does not have the answer, but they may suspect that the church is a place where they could ask the question.

Meaning and Identity

True skeptics may also discover that they need a place to ask unanswerable questions. They realize that the more urgent the question, the less likely it is to have an answer, but still they feel driven to ask questions as they try to make sense out of their lives.

William Temple, a former Archbishop of Canterbury, wrote in 1943 that the primary business of Christianity is making sense of the world, "not meaning that we can show that it makes sense, but with the more literal and radical meaning of making into sense what, till it is transformed, is largely nonsense." A skeptical person with intellectual integrity is not likely to observe that life is largely nonsense and let the matter drop there. Such a person is likely to feel compelled to pursue the business of trying to make sense out of the nonsense.

That quest, however, may best be pursued in the company of other people with a similar concern. Working alone and without challenge or support, the person on a quest for meaning easily falls prey to self delusion and conceit. The never-ending quest can also become an unbearably lonely one without companions along the way. A church that appears to be engaged in the business of looking for meaning may well be attractive even to people who know they could never believe what church members are supposed to believe.

Closely related to this desire for meaning is the need for a sense of personal identity. In an earlier age, a person's name reflected a clear identity derived from family lineage, occupation, or geography, but for most people this is no longer the case.

Names long ago lost much of their capacity to convey identity, and that may be a good thing for the majority. People are less restricted in their possibilities if their names suggest nothing about their origins. In this country many people have shortened or Anglicized their names to remove all trace of ethnic origin so that they can move around more easily in our homogenized society. Many people are also reluctant to identify themselves by their occupations. "I don't want people to know I am a lawyer when they first meet me," one successful attorney asserted. "I want them to know me as a person before they try to fit me into their preconception of what lawyers are like. There is a lot more to me than my law practice." Geography has also lost its value in providing a sense of self. For someone living in Washington, DC, having been born in Marion, Ohio, may be more a source of embarrassment than a source of identity.

The price of freedom from too close an identification with family, place of origin, and work has proved to be higher than some people are able to pay. If none of the traditional ways of identifying yourself is valid, you can lose all sense of self. The theologian Paul Tillich observed that the source of deepest dread is the threat of non-being. The stress and anxiety experienced by urban people may to some extent be the result of living constantly with the threat of being nothing. If you cannot say with confidence who you are, you may be driven either to invent a self or to repress the anxiety with sex, drugs, or some other kind of addictive behavior.

Skeptical people may sense that church members do not suffer the same loss of identity as that experienced by the general population. The language used by Christians may not have immediate appeal for skeptics, but Christians have a particular way of defining themselves that provides them with a clear identity. They call themselves children of God and fellow heirs with Christ, terms that suggest their identity has not been limited by occupation, family, or place of origin.

Reassurance

Even with a clear sense of identity, urban dwellers can suffer from disabling attacks of anxiety and stress. Anxiety and stress may always have been part of what it is to be human. What is different for people living in cities today is that they may have no way in which to shore up their confidence and their courage.

A recent college graduate came to Washington to look for a job in the federal government. She trod the corridors of public buildings from the Capitol to the Department of Agriculture for three weeks without finding anyone willing to consider her for a position. She felt defeated and frightened at the prospect of long-term unemployment. What made her situation almost unbearable, she said, was that she had no one to reassure her that she was a valuable person. She had a strong recollection of having had similar fears as a child, but when she was afraid, her father would take her in his arms for a moment or two, and then she would be ready go out and try again. In her first weeks in the city, the only time another human being touched her was when someone on the subway roughly shoved her aside to get the seat for which she was heading.

Although during college the aspiring civil servant had developed a healthy skepticism about Christianity, in her desperation she went looking for a church. It was the one place she could think of where she could allow herself to feel like a child again. She no longer believed in God, but she could pretend that God was a father who would put his arms around her for a few moments until she felt stronger. She also knew that in an Episcopal Church there was a place in the service called "The Peace" when people shook hands or even embraced the people next to them. That human touch along with the fantasy about the arms of God could help her find her courage.

Longing for God

Skeptics, by definition, are people who are not convinced that a relationship with God is possible. They are not willing, however, to assert that God does not exist. Skeptics are likely to find themselves in sympathy with the religious reflections of Albert Einstein. Einstein could not conceive of a personal God that rewards and punishes its creatures, but he expressed a "rapturous amazement at the harmony of natural law, which reveals an intelligence of such superiority that, compared with it, all the systematic thinking and acting of human beings is an utterly insignificant reflection."

Given the possibility of a superior intelligence at work in the universe, skeptics at critical junctures in their lives often long to be in harmony with whatever that superior intelligence may be. For Einstein the crisis was his awareness of the mystery of the universe: "One has been endowed with just enough intelligence to be able to see clearly how utterly inadequate that intelligence is when confronted with what exists." For a friend of mine, the occasion was the death of his father from whom he had been estranged for over twenty years. The mystery of love and hate, of parent and child, of life and death made him aware of his longing for God.

For a skeptic to claim belief in God might be dishonest, but to deny a longing for God could be an equally false claim. Simone Weil suggested that the great blasphemy is not in doubting that God exists but in making believe that the hunger is not real.

In order to live with integrity, a skeptic may be forced to admit a longing for God. The question then arises, "How do you find a legitimate way to express such a longing?" It may be that the church is a place where people gather, not so much to acknowledge their convictions about God, but to confess their deepest desire to be in harmony with the superior intelligence that lies behind the mystery of existence.

A Few Words for Episcopalians

Skeptical people with previous experience in the Episcopal Church are a special case. Being exposed to the Episcopal Church as a child can be like being exposed to chicken pox; you may be immune to the experience as an adult. If you are sufficiently intrigued to have read this far, however, the chances are that your immunity is wearing off. Although you may be becoming open once again to what the Episcopal Church has to offer, you face a certain problem not experienced by those skeptics who do not suffer the disadvantage of premature participation.

The problem suffered by former Episcopalians is an excess of nostalgia for the pre-1979 church. Although they left the church when they found that the services were boring and discovered that they did not believe a word of it, they were never able to discard completely an aesthetic attachment to the forms of ritual. When nostalgia for the church of their childhood draws them back, they are often shocked and offended by what they see and hear. They cannot find their place in the once–familiar Book of Common Prayer. They are confused by references to such options as Rites One and Two and Eucharistic Prayers A, B, C, and D. They may be put off by being touched physically at the place of a novel intrusion into their private reflections referred to as "The Peace". They may be repelled by the presence of women clergy at the altar. Although they still find the service boring and still do not believe a word of it, they are likely to feel betrayed because the church has made changes during their absence. I understand the feeling. I always felt out of place in the small Nebraska grade school I attended as a child, but I was outraged when the townspeople decided to tear it down and build a modern facility. Unhappy as I was there, I wanted the possibility of going back whenever I felt like being in touch with my roots.

Having an aesthetic attachment to the church as it was before 1979 can be real barrier to finding something of moral and religious value for a former Episcopalian who returns as an adult skeptic. An aesthetic attachment to the present-day church can also be a barrier to moral and religious development, for that matter, but the problem usually emerges as nostalgia for the old forms. If this is your problem, and you want to explore the possibilities of returning to the church as a skeptic, you have to recognize how aesthetics can function as a barrier.

The difficulty of encountering the church at the level of aesthetics is that the participant becomes limited by the feelings stirred up by the sights and sounds of the worship. The aesthete becomes so enamored of the emotions touched by the color, the movement, and the music that consciousness of moral dilemmas or ultimate questions becomes an impossibility. I hate to say it, but former Episcopalians who want to find something of moral and religious value for themselves as skeptical adults may just have to suffer through the new forms until they become familiar with them. The only other option is to find a church that has refused to change, but those churches tend to be quite inhospitable to non-believers.

Many Episcopalians could probably be classified as semi-believers or semi-skeptics. They go to church at least two or three Sundays a month, they make regular financial contributions, and they attend social functions, but they have problems with some of the language in the worship. Most of the time the words do not worry them, but if they stop to think about the meaning of what they are hearing and saying, they are occasionally troubled. Was Jesus really "born of the Virgin Mary"? Did he actually rise again from the dead? They would be reluctant to say so without expressing some reservations, but they are not sure that talking about their reservations is appropriate in church.

In the more genteel past, I was acquainted with Episcopalians who knew themselves to be skeptics at heart but were untroubled by their skepticism. When I was a newly-ordained curate, I was once stopped on the street by a crusty old retired colonel who demanded to know why there were so few young people in church. I supposed the reason was that they could not believe all the things the church taught. "Believe?" he protested. "It has nothing to do with believing. A gentleman's duty is to attend church every Sunday." In that era, many people in the pews of the Episcopal Church on Sunday mornings were unconcerned about the lack of congruity between their personal convictions and the language of the prayer book, but times changed and incongruity became identified with phoniness. Many people who thought their church participation was phony solved the problem by leaving, but others stayed and have tried to cope with the disparity they feel between what the church teaches and what they actually believe.

Making the church a hospitable place for honest skeptics is a goal for some clergy and lay leaders in the church. Although this book does not address the question of mission strategy among these people directly, it may prove to be a useful tool in opening up the traditions and resources of the Episcopal Church to people who are unable to become true believers.

Skeptics, especially those who are well educated and reasonably affluent, are probably the most appropriate target population for the mission of the Episcopal Church. One reason for concentrating on these people is that our cities are full of them and the other churches do not want them unless they are willing to become believers, something many of them simply cannot do. Episcopalians have had a long tradition of accepting a variety of opinions on nearly every subject. For the most part, they have put more stress on behavior and on form than on belief. In *Constant Circle*, a book about H. L. Mencken and his friends, Sara Mayfield reported that both her father and Mencken's wife favored the Episcopal Church because "it doesn't interfere with people's religion or their politics, either." It is in that spirit, I think, that the Episcopal Church should reach out to people who are looking for something in the church but who do not want to be told what to believe.

Another reason for reaching out to skeptics is that these people are much like those presently attending Episcopal churches. "Like attracts like in evangelism," according to sociologist Dean Hoge of Catholic University. "Most people join churches because of personal relationships with existing members." As recent surveys show, the Episcopal Church currently draws most of its membership from the same kind of people who make up the vast majority of intelligent, educated skeptics. Too many leaders in the Episcopal Church have been overly impressed by the success of conservative churches, which has led to a fundamental error in mission strategy.

Some of them have supposed that, because the fundamentalist and pentecostal churches are growing while the membership of the Episcopal Church remains static at best, Episcopalians are rejecting their heritage in favor of right-wing Christianity. They note that although the membership of the Episcopal Church stays about the same, approximately 40% of the members grew up in another tradition. From these figures they conclude that the Episcopal Church must be losing 40% of its people to the conservative churches. According to Hoge this is a false assumption: "Few people leave the Episcopal Church for fundamentalist or pentecostal congregations. Most of the Episcopalians who leave the church do so because they want to attend church with their spouses who belong to other denominations or because they no longer want to attend church at all."

Because they have been envious of the success of the conservative churches, some Episcopalians have adopted the style and theology of the fundamentalists and pentecostals. By appealing to people who demand simple answers to complex questions and who prefer slogans to thinking their way through issues, however, they abandon their natural constituency. It is true that a few of the Episcopal churches that have taken this route have become enormously successful in attracting hordes of new members. For the most part, these congregations behave like Baptist churches or Assemblies of God, the only differences being that the clergy wear traditional vestments and that a portion of the service comes from the prayer book. The members they attract generally are suburbanites who are looking for a church that is upscale but reminds them of the religion they knew in their youth. Many want to be in a large church where the numbers of people around them convince them that they have found the right answers.

Although the results of this limited ministry have been impressive, few church leaders seem willing to look at the price the rest of the church has to pay for their success. They are pushing the church to take stands on issues like abortion and national defense that make the church as a whole less and less inviting to liberals as well as to honest skeptics.

My intention is not simply to condemn the neo-conservative Episcopalians, but rather to suggest that the rest of the church focus its missionary energy on its natural constituency, the educated and intelligent skeptics who inhabit our urban areas in large numbers. My hope is that this book which is intended for their reading might also be useful to the church leaders who want to work with them.

Aelred Graham, an English Benedictine monk who made a study of Eastern religions, once told me that every belief system was like a finger pointing to the moon. People waste their time concentrating on the differences among the fingers instead of looking toward the moon itself. I have no interest in trying to prove that my understanding of the Anglican tradition is the correct one. Nor for that matter do I have any desire to promote Christianity, or the Episcopal Church's representation of Christianity, as the only true religion. Rather I am trying to find ways for skeptical people to look at what is true without being side-tracked by arguments about the fingers we use to point at the truth.

Chapter 2
THE NATURE OF BELIEVING

In a series of lectures at Oxford University on St. Paul's Epistle to the Romans, Robert Morgan came to chapter ten, verse nine and read:

> ... if you confess with your lips that Jesus is Lord and believe in your heart that God raised him from the dead, you will be saved.

Then he looked up and said, "Believe in your heart. That is the only kind of believing that matters. As you probably know the Latin word *credo*, from which we get our word 'creed', is usually translated 'believe', but it means literally 'to set the heart'."

I was stunned. My real reason for spending a six-month sabbatical at Oxford was to study Celtic Christianity. I had been sitting in on the Romans lectures simply because I had met Bob Morgan and had found him to be a bright and interesting person, one from whom I thought I might learn something, but I had not been prepared for this sudden solution to a vexing problem: how can a skeptical person say the Nicene Creed with integrity? *Credo*, translated into English as "I believe in", really means "I set my heart". It does not mean "I set my head". It does not mean "I hold these opinions although they are unsupported or even contradicted by empirical evidence".

This was too good to be true. I was afraid to place too much reliance on the words of one scholar so I rushed out of the lecture hall to look for a Latin dictionary in the Pusey Theological Library. I found one and quickly turned to *credo*. The definition: "to set the heart". If I had only known enough to look before, I would not have needed a Latin dictionary; my battered college edition of Webster's would have been sufficient. The entry for creed includes the information that the word is derived from the Latin *credo*, which in turn comes from the Indo-European root *cred*, heart + *dhe*, to place. A little time with the dictionaries showed me that these same roots form both the Greek and Latin words for "heart". The

Greek word for heart is *kardia* and the Latin is *core; cordis* in
the genitive case. All early Christians who spoke either Greek
or Latin, as most of them did, would have known that when
they said the creed they were talking about matters of the heart.

When the Latin-speaking missionaries were presenting
Christianity to the English in the early seventh century, they
discovered that "heart" had no verb form in the English language. If Christianity were arriving in America for the first
time today, the absence of a suitable verb would present no
problem. Any society that can accept "parent" and "dialogue"
as verbs would surely have no problem with "heart", but thir-
teen hundred years ago the Roman missionaries did not think
they could translate the creed to begin "I heart one God". They
had to find another word with connotations that were similar
to those of "credo", which could mean "to give as a loan" or
"to have confidence in someone or something" or "to trust".
In English the phrase "to believe in" conveys some of those
same thoughts. That would have been fair enough, but what
has made life in the English-speaking church difficult for skeptics is the custom of translating the Latin *opinor* with the
phrase "to believe that". *Opinor*, from which we get our word
"opinion", originally meant to suppose or imagine. Few
people have a sufficiently developed sensitivity for language to
recognize the difference in meaning when in as opposed to
that follows the verb "believe". As a consequence, not many
know when the church is speaking about matters of the heart
as opposed to the things of the mind.

The Heart and the Mind

The confusion over the nature of believing can cause unnecessary anguish for skeptics, especially when they most need
and long for God. When they associate believing with the work-
ings of their minds instead of their hearts, they think that they
have no right to approach God. At the same time they may
feel ashamed that they are unable to repress their desire for
God, a longing that they cannot reconcile with a rational view
of the universe. The cosmic loneliness mingled with shame
often surfaces in the words and behavior of skeptics as bitterness or anger. That was certainly the case with Dorothy, a
forty-eight-year-old pediatrician who was dying of cancer.

Although Dorothy had attended Sunday school as a child, she had been a thorough-going skeptic since her sophomore year in college. Yet in spite of her continued skepticism, she began going to church again a few years after a messy and painful divorce. She was lonely and miserable and thought that the church might be a place where she could make some new friends. In church she quickly gravitated toward a group of divorced and widowed women of about her own age who met for an hour each Sunday before the worship service. Gradually she recovered much of the self-esteem that had been seriously eroded by her failed marriage, and she began to feel optimistic about the future. Just when she felt fully restored, she received a devastating blow from an unexpected quarter: cancer in her pancreas.

For several months, Dorothy carried on as if nothing were the matter. She told her group at church about the diagnosis but refused to discuss the matter further. In my presence she did not admit the seriousness of her illness until the day she asked me to come visit her at home.

"I found out yesterday that I only have a few more weeks, maybe only days," she said. "Since you are the rector of my church you will have to do my funeral, and you should know that I don't believe in God and I don't believe in heaven." I did not say anything, so she went on. "How can I believe in God when I've had to watch little children die? There was nothing I could do to save them, and they hadn't done anything to deserve what was happening to them. I've had to treat children who were horribly beaten by their own parents and mangled in automobile accidents caused by drunk drivers. How can anybody believe in a God that allows such terrible things to happen to innocent children?"

Dorothy's words showed that she was using "believe" as an action of the mind, but the anger in her voice as well as the nature of her complaint demonstrated what it can mean to believe in the heart. When she reflected on the implications of what she had said, she realized that while she could not intellectually accept most of the conventional opinions about God, she could admit that she had set her heart on God. As she faced death, she longed to be in relationship to God. Although she remained skeptical to the end, by the time she died she had nevertheless developed the confidence that God could accept her anger, mistrust, and disappointment.

Dorothy died with the confidence that God accepted her. That may be what it means to believe in the heart.

The Limits of Logic

By the time Christianity got to Britain, Roman Christians could make a distinction between the functions of the mind and the heart. They could, but I am not sure they always did. In all probability they did not use "heart" exclusively as a metaphor suggesting the emotions as we do today.

They may have been much closer to the Greek-speaking Christians of the first century in that regard. When St. Paul wrote in Greek about "believing in the heart", *kardia* had a variety of meanings, some of which seem to be contradictory by today's standards. Paul could have been using *kardia* as the seat of emotional or of mental life. He could have considered the heart to be the center of feeling or of thinking. He could have seen the heart as the source of grief, desire, and love, or he could have equated the heart with the mind.

From all the contexts in which *kardia* appears in the literature of the time before and during the life of St. Paul, however, it never seems to refer to logic or analysis. In fact, St. Paul in writing to the church in Philippi makes a clear declaration that he places little weight on the intellect in the matter of a person's relationship to God, and that he can make a distinction between heart and mind:

> And the peace of God, which passes all understanding, will keep your hearts and minds in Christ Jesus.

The word here translated as "understanding" refers to the functioning of the intellect. "Passes" in Greek is a more dynamic word than it sounds; it actually means passes through, in the sense of "break through". We could accurately paraphrase Paul's words by saying that "the peace of God, which breaks through the logical constructions you place on life, will guard both your hearts and your minds, that is, your feeling and your thinking." Although scholars can argue about what St. Paul really meant when he wrote "believe in your heart", I think skeptics are on solid ground if they understand these words to mean "having emotions", particularly a longing for God, rather than holding opinions about God that cannot be supported by empirical evidence. Unfortunately for skeptics, however, an emphasis on accepting intellectual propositions about God has tended to dominate Christian theology in many periods of history.

As a consequence of this emphasis on intellectual propositions, skeptics may never have come across the writings of the numerous faithful Christians who emphasized what it means to believe in the heart, such as the author of *The Cloud of Unknowing*. In the fourteenth century an anonymous monk in the north of England wrote a little book on contemplative prayer that picks up the early Christian concept of finding God in your heart rather than with your intellect. Although the great learning demonstrated in his book shows that he was not anti-intellectual, he was keenly aware of the limits of logic in approaching God. He taught that contemplative prayer was hard work because when you seek God what you first find is darkness, "as it were a cloud of unknowing". If ever you are going to feel God's presence, "it behoveth always to be in this cloud." As the anonymous monk continues his instructions for those seeking God, he writes:

> . . . all reasonable creatures, angel and man, have in them each by himself, one principal working power, the which is called a knowledgeable power, and the other working power, the which is called a loving power. Of the which two powers, to the first, the which is a knowledgeable power, God that is the maker of them is evermore incomprehensible; and to the second, the which is the loving power, in each one diversely He is all comprehensible to the full.

If skeptics with a longing for God can accept the guidance of this fourteenth-century English monk, they can put aside the notion that Christian believing would require them to engage in acts that are intellectually dishonest. Believing as described in *The Cloud of Unknowing* is a willingness to acknowledge the limits of reason and knowledge and to affirm the power of love that opens the self to God's presence.

In asserting that God cannot be comprehended through knowledge, the Englishman who wrote *The Cloud* was following a well-established tradition in the church, one that has been especially cherished in Anglican Christianity. In the ninth century a Scot known as Johannes Scotus Erigena had pondered the impossibility of comprehending God by means of the intellect. He wrote:

> We do not know what God is. God himself does not know what He is because He is not anything. Literally, God is not, because He transcends being.

Many modern skeptics may be surprised to learn that throughout the ages respected Christian theologians have been in on the secret. From an intellectual point of view, "God is not". Both the ninth-century Scot and the fourteenth-century English monk were strongly influenced by a group of writings that had been circulating in the church since the fifth century and was at one time attributed to Dionysius the Areopagite, a disciple of St. Paul mentioned in the Acts of the Apostles. Although most modern skeptics would probably not find everything in the collection congenial to their way of thinking, they might find their point of view affirmed by a strand of thought that runs through the little book called "The Divine Names". The book raises the question, "How, then, can God possibly be a being?" and answers the question by asserting:

> He neither was, nor will be, nor became, nor is becoming, nor will become; rather He is not; but he is the "to be" of all beings.

God is not because the mind simply cannot comprehend the one whom the heart longs to love. The heart, however, cannot operate without the mind, hence the need for the divine names.

This strand of thinking in the church—that God cannot be comprehended by the mind—can be traced back through Clement of Alexandria in the second century. He may have been the first Christian to articulate the need for religious language to express matters of the heart, which cannot be put into logical form:

> The deity is without form and nameless. Though we ascribe names, they are not to be taken in their strict meaning: when we call him one, good, mind, existence, Father, God, creator, Lord, we are not conferring a name on him. Being unable to do more, we use these appellations of honor in order that our thought may have something to rest on.

Christians use their minds to find ways of talking about what they can only know in their hearts, but they must always remember that their ideas about God do not describe God.

The words associated with God are useful because their thoughts need "something to rest on", but they do not use these words in the same way as they would when they are talking about history, science, or current events. Skeptics who are able to adopt this point of view often find that Christianity becomes a real possibility for them. They can learn to use the words as they would in poetry and in psychology. The words are evidence of feelings rather than of thoughts. The language of religion is the language of the heart rather than of the mind.

Faith and Believing

The confusion created in using the English word "believe" in the translation of the creed extends to translations of the Bible. In his letters, St. Paul frequently used two words from the same root: the verb *pisteuo* and the noun pistis. The noun can properly be translated as "faithfulness, reliability, trust, confidence, faith". The verb, usually translated "believe", meant either to give credence to what someone said or to have confidence or trust in the person. You see the problem. In English we have no simple verbs to express faithfulness, reliability, trust, confidence, or faith so we are stuck with awkward phrases or forced to use the word that is the source of so much trouble for skeptics: believe. I prefer using the awkward phrases, because in so doing I think we can actually get closer to what St. Paul and the other early Christians meant, and we can open up the practice of Christianity to skeptical people.

With the original meanings of the key words in mind, we can return to St. Paul's advice to the Christians in Rome:

> . . . if you confess with your lips that Jesus is Lord and believe in your heart that God raised him from the dead, you will be saved.

What St. Paul may have been talking about was having confidence in God, a trust in God identified with the story told about Jesus, for whom death was not the last word. From my reading of the passage, I think St. Paul was almost surely not saying: "If you can intellectually accept as a fact of history— without a shred of reliable evidence—that Jesus was resuscitated after being dead for three days, you will get whatever God has to offer." I do not think St. Paul was telling the

Romans that if they could convince themselves that they knew what they could not possibly know, because they were not present at the time, God would hold them in special regard. On the contrary, I think St. Paul was talking about the reliability of the evidence they had in their hearts. They could have confidence in the Jesus story because from their own experience they knew in their hearts about the possibility of being raised to new life when they felt as if their lives had ended.

Carl held a political appointment in the Department of Commerce. As a top level economist he had direct access to the Secretary and frequently prepared position papers for the White House. He loved his work, but he had frequent policy disputes with the Secretary, whose views were much more conservative than his own. The under-secretary, who was nominally his direct superior, warned him a few times that he should try to minimize his differences with the boss, but he paid little attention until the day when he found a brief note in his box letting him know that his services were no longer required by the federal government.

He was stunned. He was also scared. Carl had a wife and three small children, a mortgage requiring hefty monthly payments, and no savings, and no obvious prospects for new employment.

After he got over his first wave of panic, Carl talked with his wife and a few close friends about what he should do next. He wondered if this might be the time to make a radical change in his career. For a long time he had cherished the idea of becoming a teacher, but because starting salaries for instructors and assistant professors were far below what he had commanded in the government and in private industry, he had never dared to pursue the possibility. Most of his closest friends, including his wife, encouraged him to use the time suddenly made available to make inquiries among his colleagues at the universities. Within three months, before many of his acquaintances even knew that he had been fired, he was established at a prestigious university, and he and his family were living in a lovely house that they could actually afford on his reduced income.

When Easter came that year, Carl knew in his heart that the story about Jesus being raised from the dead was a true story because it was a story he had just lived through. Although he could never say with certainty that God had intervened in his life, he could and did say that is what the experience felt like. He decided to live the rest of his life as if God had raised him up from the lowest point to which he had ever fallen.

Carl's new life was possible because he had acquired the confidence that something of value could arise from any disaster that might overtake him. That may be exactly what St. Paul had in mind when he urged the Christians in Rome to have confidence in their hearts that God raised Jesus from the dead.

Faith as Affirmation

Probably the most often-quoted passage from St. Paul's writings in which he uses the word faith, or *pistis*, appears near the beginning of his Letter to the Romans: "He who through faith (*pistis*) is righteous shall live." Here Paul is quoting the Old Testament prophet Habakkuk, whose word for "faith" was formed from a root that produced a word still in use today: *amen*. It was such an important word in the teaching of Jesus that when the gospels were written in Greek, the authors did not translate it. Most people today are familiar with the formula Jesus used to attract attention to something important he was going to say. "Verily, verily" or "truly, truly" appear frequently in our English versions, but the words in the Greek original are "amen, amen". Amen is an affirmation; it means "yes". Originally then, faith had something to do with an affirmation of what is, a "yes" to the facts as we know them about our universe and about ourselves.

Habakkuk and St. Paul both taught that righteousness was the result of faith. To understand what they meant, we need to look at the word "righteousness". Literally it meant "uprightness", a metaphor derived from the observation that posts set at right angles to the ground to support roof beams could carry more weight than those leaning to one side. An upright person, then, was one who appeared to be strong and steady, able to bear great burdens. To achieve that condition people needed faith, that is, the capacity to accept the reality of the world around them and within them. That insight may fit with the experience of most skeptics: people who face the facts about their situation and about their own feelings possess strengths unknown to people who try to cope with their sorrows and anxieties by pretense and self-delusion.

A colleague of mine was extremely upset. Although he was an ordained clergyman, a local church had hired him to work as a community organizer in the housing projects that adjoin the neighborhood. He proved to be an excellent organizer, working well with a variety of church and civic organizations whose efforts he coordinated. In spite of his success, however, he appeared to be quite unhappy. One day he complained to a group of clergy, "I came here to work with people, but I spend all of my time arranging meetings, filling out grant applications, buying supplies for the summer youth program, getting the bus repaired, and keeping the books. I'm not a minister anymore. I'm just an administrator."

One of the clergymen, who greatly admired and appreciated his work, gently asked in response to this outburst, "Who asked you to pick up on all this administrative detail?"

"Nobody asked me. It just had to be done."

"I thought when you came here two years ago you were given the freedom to write your own job description and to do whatever you thought was important. I wonder how it happened that you took over so many of the administrative details for all of the neighborhood organizations."

The community organizer was quiet for several moments. Then he said, "I guess I must sort of like administration. I know I'm good at it, but I always thought ministers were supposed to prefer working directly with people, so I have been thinking that I am pretty much of a failure."

With the help of his colleagues, he finally began to face some of the facts about himself that he had been denying: he was a shy person, often uncomfortable with close inter-personal contact; he was a gifted administrator; he had created a job for himself that suited his talents; he was admired and appreciated by his colleagues and the community he served. Having said "yes" to the facts, his gloom lifted. Or to put it in biblical terms, when he responded to his situation with faith, he found he could stand upright with the burden of the community on his shoulders.

Faith and Doubt

While believing, in the usual sense of the word today, may not be a possibility for skeptics, faith of the kind described in the Bible may. Unfortunately, many people use "faith" in ways that are quite non-biblical, usually ones that suggest the absence of doubt. People said of a woman in my home town: "What tremendous faith she has! She never doubted for a moment that her son would recover from brain cancer." In this context, faith seems to imply the capacity to predict the future. The mother claimed to know the outcome of her son's illness. In a different context, faith seems to be the equivalent of stubbornness: "There goes a man of real faith. He believes the world was created just as it is written in the Bible." Such a man is more stubborn than faithful; he simply refuses to examine the abundant evidence that suggests the biblical story belongs to the category of myth, or to accept the scientific data that proves the earth was formed millions of years ago.

Because of the way many believers use the word "faith", many skeptics think that the opposite of faith is doubt and that doubt is unacceptable in church. As far as the Episcopal Church is concerned, however, that is a misconception. Even without a full awareness of the Hebrew concept of faith that entered the Christian tradition, most Episcopalians sense that the opposite of amen is not doubt but denial. To be faithless is to deny the reality of what you know about yourself and about the world around you. If you think of faith as the affirmation of reality, then doubt is not the opposite of faith but an essential ingredient of faith. To doubt is to raise questions about what does not make sense to you. To doubt is to weigh the evidence for yourself when you think people are drawing erroneous conclusions. In my experience of the Episcopal Church, it is a place where the questions are welcome and the weighing of evidence encouraged. Visitors are not required to park their critical faculties at the church door.

Once skeptics start voicing their doubts in church, they may be in for a surprise. Skeptics often discover the questions that have troubled them for a long time are relatively unimportant

for church people, for example, the "facts" surrounding the
resurrection of Jesus. In probably the most-well known story
about doubting in the New Testament, Thomas refuses to accept the report of his fellow disciples about a visit from the
risen Lord. In examining this passage from the Gospel according to St. John, Northrop Frye in *The Great Code*, observes:

> When the apostle Thomas demanded visible and tangible
> evidence for the Resurrection, he was told that he would
> have understood the Resurrection more clearly if he hadn't
> bothered with it. I doubt that the implication of this story is
> that an uncritical attitude is spiritually closer to the truth than
> a critical one. I think that the implication is rather that the
> more trustworthy the evidence the more misleading it is.

The evidence offered to prove that the resurrection of Jesus
was a historical event is simply irrelevant. A skeptic has a perfect right even in church to question the evidence offered in
the Bible or by such artifacts as the Shroud of Turin. Doubting the reliability of such claims is useful because in asking the
questions the skeptics can learn to move beyond the trivial to
the basic reality, which they can affirm. They can learn to set
aside the misleading evidence of the resurrection and to say
"yes" to the their own experience and to the evidence of resurrection found in their hearts.

The Centrality of Paradox

Although understanding faith as affirmation of reality can
open up the possibilities of Christianity for some skeptics, the
concept presents a fairly basic problem: one perception of
reality may be in absolute conflict with another equally valid
perception. Just look at the folk wisdom many people absorbed as children:

> "Look before you leap" is good advice, but do not forget
> that "he who hesitates is lost."
> "Watch the pennies and the dollars will take care of them-
> selves" may be an accurate statement, but what happens to
> the people who are "penny wise and pound foolish"?

Most skeptics are skeptical when presented with what is supposed to be a profound truth because they have learned that
for every profound truth there is an equal and opposite truth.
The opposite of an insignificant truth may be a lie, but the opposite of an ultimate truth is always another truth. Two such

opposing truths are called a paradox, literally, truths alongside each other. Paradox is basic to skepticism, but what many skeptics do not realize is that paradox is also basic to Christianity.

To begin with, no more paradoxical collection of writings can be found than the Hebrew Scriptures. When I was young, some humanists were trying to hold the Bible up to ridicule by pointing out all of the contradictions they could find in it. Apparently they have now given up the game in the realization that they were producing the opposite reaction from the one they intended: they were undergirding confidence in the Bible because contradictions are evidence of wisdom. The Jews who assembled the Bible were very wise to include two creation stories. In the first chapter of Genesis male and female human beings appear simultaneously and without any mention of differences between the two sexes, a reminder of a profound truth: men and women are the same and deserve equal treatment. In the second and third chapters of Genesis, however, we find another story that emphasizes the differences between a man and a woman, a reminder of the opposite truth: male and female human beings have different physical characteristics and different requirements. The pattern continues through the subsequent chapters and books. For every important truth identified in the Hebrew Scriptures, an opposite truth lurks about waiting to be discovered.

Jesus continued his teaching in the Hebrew tradition of affirming paradox:

"Many that are first will be last and the last first."

"Whoever will save his life will lose it."

St. Paul also followed the pattern of paradox with statements such as:

"It is no longer I who live, but Christ who lives in me."

"When I am weak, then I am strong."

The concept of paradox remained central to many Christian theologians over the centuries who discovered that pressing contradictions as far as they were able opened their intuitions to the presence of God. As Aelred Graham wrote, such theologians understood God as "the coincidence of opposites, wherein all contradictions meet."

The contradictions that can open the way to God may arise in even the most mundane human situations. The conflicting forces, experienced as desires and fears, represent moral values. Here are a few of samples of the kind of internal paradox that managers in business—as well as volunteer community leaders—have to face:

> When I chair a meeting, I want to give everyone the opportunity to express opinions, and I want to cover all the agenda items on time.When I assign responsibility to experts, I want to trust them in areas where I have little experience, but I want to keep on top of all the jobs for which I am responsible. When people under my supervision fail, I want to give honest, negative criticism, but I do not want to undermine their self-confidence.

The movement from these internal paradoxes to an experience of faith follows a fairly predictable route. Look back at the first of the three management issues and picture Mel, the president of the citizens association in a residential community, presiding at the monthly meeting. The community center is packed; half of the people are standing or sitting on the floor because the chairs were all taken a quarter of an hour before the meeting began. The unusual attendance was obviously precipitated by a proposal of the board of directors to change the zoning of a tract near the center of the village to permit the construction of a large office building. Most of the residents want to keep the community as it is, but many of the people active in community affairs want to expand the tax base so they can improve police and fire protection. Everyone seems to have something to say about the controversy, but Mel and the board want to complete the whole meeting agenda, including reports on the schools and security problems and the state of the treasury, before 10:00 p.m. and before tempers explode in rage.

Think about Mel looking out over a sea of angry faces and waving hands—with motions, and motions to amend the motions, and motions to table the motions clogging up the legislative machinery—as he experienced the conflicts let loose by the community meeting. Every time he allowed someone to speak, he was delaying the meeting. Every time he tried to bring matters to a vote, he was denying people the right to express their opinions. He was in despair, to use the word in its original meaning, that is, without hope. He could not hope to please everyone; he could not hope to have the meeting end on a happy note. At each moment in the meeting, Mel had to decide if he was going to let someone speak or make an attempt at moving on. He had his board at the head table with him and he had a parliamentarian, but he alone had to decide in each instance what to do.

After the meeting, if Mel wanted to be reflective, he could have looked back at his behavior and discovered some clues as to the nature of his religion. The solitude provided by his own house that evening would have been his first opportunity to examine the kind of faith by which he operated. Most people cannot recognize faith under the pressure of a given moment; faith is discernable only in retrospect. In retrospect Mel might have recognized his lord, that is, who or what held his life together. A few of the many possible "lords" in Mel's life might be:

—The shot of bourbon he had before the meeting and the double martini he was anticipating. Alcohol can mask the despair and make it tolerable.

—His success as an attorney. He would recognize this lord by recalling that he favored clients and colleagues at the expense of other members of the community.

—His popularity. As president, he had ample opportunity to push for the board decision instead of chairing the meeting in an even-handed manner.

—Money. Five years ago he had purchased two lots near the shopping center on speculation. If zoning changes allow for an increase in commercial activity, the lots would soon be worth double their current value. If he had done everything possible to put through the proposed change, he might conclude that money shapes his life.

—His wife. The woman he married loved their peaceful community and did not want anything to change. Pleasing her was the only way he could find any peace. Being out of favor meant cold coffee and burned toast and no sex, so if his wife were his lord he would have tried to block the commerical interests to the best of his ability.

—God, as represented by Jesus of Nazareth. If this were the case, he would see that he had done his best to affirm the reality of his situation, including the paradox within himself. He would understand that in the complexity of the situation no clearly right decisions were possible. He would accept what he had done as being simply the best he was capable of doing at the time, knowing that in some of his decisions he had been unfair because he had been unduly influenced by personal values, which he had done his best to keep from being competing "lords" in his life. He would identify as gifts of God whatever wisdom he had demonstrated and whatever strength had kept him from coming apart as he was pulled by the conflicting interests present in the meeting.

The last option represents one way for skeptics to practice Christianity, a way that has biblical and historical roots. Robert Browning once wrote of "a paradox which comforts while it mocks". That phrase indicates to me the kind of faith possible for a skeptic. By affirming the mockery that each paradox makes of human existence, skeptics may come to experience the only dependable sort of comfort available in this life.

Faith: A Gift Not Everybody Gets

Although I have tried to open up the concept of believing so that faith can become a possibility for skeptics, I do not want to imply that faith is necessary for skeptics who want to practice Christianity. Apparently at some time in his life St. Paul was of a similar opinion. In the twelfth chapter of his First Letter to the Corinthians, he wrote:

> To each is given the manifestation of the Spirit for the common good. To one is given through the Spirit the utterance of wisdom, and to another the utterance of knowledge by the same Spirit, to another faith (*pistis*) by the same Spirit, to another gifts of healing by the one Spirit, to another the working of miracles . . . .

Whatever Paul meant by *pistis*, he seems to think of it as a gift that not everyone receives. This passage has been particularly troubling to some Christian believers. How could a member of the Christian community not have faith? They have tried to explain away the more likely meaning by saying that here (and only here) Paul is speaking about the special kind of faith required in order to be eligible for the next two gifts on the list—healing and miracle working—but that is not what he says. He makes as great a distinction between healing and faith as he does between faith and knowledge, the preceding category. Paul must have been using *pistis* to convey one of its usual meanings. We are left with the following possibilities:

First, not everyone receives the gift of faithfulness or reliability. That observation tallies with my experience. Some people with the gifts of wisdom or knowledge or healing are unreliable. They are late for appointments and do not finish work they promise to do.

Second, not everyone receives the gift of confidence or trust. That also seems true. No matter how hard they try, some people just cannot trust God. God seems to be elusive and undependable, and no amount of will power is sufficient to make them feel confident or trusting.

Third, not everyone receives the capacity for accepting the truth of opinions unsupported by verifiable evidence. Stated this way, the passage still makes sense. Some people have critical minds and simply cannot help analyzing and testing the available data, while other people can believe almost anything. Everyday the newspapers print horoscopes and millions of people base critical decisions on this unverifiable information. Some scientists have espoused the healing power of vitamin C or an extract of peach pits, even though all carefully controlled studies have failed to verify such theories. Many aspects of the "New Age" religions have captured the imaginations of apparently intelligent people. They are prepared to believe reports of harmonic convergence, astral voyaging, channeling, manual lymph drainage, and the mystical property of crystals, but not everyone is capable of such belief.

Fourth, not everyone receives the ability to affirm reality. That statement is true as well. Certainly many people cannot accept what they perceive to be true, especially when the truths they perceive contradict one another.

My conclusion, therefore, is that Paul is making an accurate statement no matter which of the accepted meanings of *pistis* we apply in trying to understand him. As far as I am concerned, that is good news for skeptics who have an interest in the church. They may not have any recognizable kind of faith, but that does not matter. People are different. Some have one kind of faith and some another, and some have no faith at all.

I am sure that I do not know how it is that some people have some kind of faith and others none at all, but I observe that such is the case. Perhaps some people are by nature born believers. Maybe it is a generic trait. Or maybe calling faith a gift of the Spirit is as good a way as any to acknowledge the mystery of how faith operates in some lives and is missing from others.

If faith is a gift that not everybody receives, then nobody has a reason for feeling guilty about not having faith and nobody can be blamed for not having faith. Skeptics who want to attend church should keep St. Paul's teaching about the gifts of the Spirit ready to offer in case they are cornered by believers who are shocked to find a skeptic in the congregation. All the skeptic has to say is, "I have many gifts, but faith doesn't seem to be one of them."

Part Two

***

Getting Past The Barriers

Skeptics may acknowledge their longing for what the church seems to offer. They may become convinced that believing is not necessary for the practice of Christianity. They may even find an Episcopal church in which they feel at home. Before they can participate whole-heartedly in the life of a Christian community, however, they must find a way to get past three formidable barriers: the Bible, the Nicene Creed, and the business of prayer.

The three chapters that follow offer the skeptic ways of coming to terms with the most difficult intellectual barriers to the practice of Christianity, but barriers raised up by disagreeable experiences may loom almost as large. These deserve some recognition. Skeptics should not attempt to deny or dismiss lightly any aspect of Christianity that appears to be a barrier.

Before dealing with the intellectual barriers, skeptics would do well to acknowledge the unpleasant encounters, such as the following, that stand between themselves and the church.

One memory that stood in the way of my returning to church as an adult was the musty smell of the church basement where I had gone to Sunday school. The room was not open from one Sunday to the next. It smelled of the damp wood-pulp paper from which our workbooks were made. It smelled of mildew in the multi-floral rugs and on the dun-colored walls. It smelled of the face powder our elderly teachers wore. It smelled of confinement and boredom. I had to get past the memory of that smell in order to go back to church.

Many people find that unpleasant memories of clergy they have known get in the way of pursuing a renewed interest in Christianity. That was true for me. I dropped out of church at age twelve because I thought the pastor had insulted me. When he told us during a confirmation class that man had been made in the image and likeness of God, my mind leapt immediately to the series of drawings in my science book depicting the evolution of human beings from Neanderthal man to the present. Taking the words "image and likeness" literally, in all innocence I asked him if God looked like a Neanderthal, or if he looked like us, or if he were constantly changing in appearance. The pastor laughed at me, in front of all my friends. In retrospect, I suppose he thought I was mocking him, but at the time I was aware only of the embarrassment he had caused me. I spoke to him just one more time. I went back to tell him I was quitting his class, but I did not tell him that the reason was that I felt insulted. I gave him another and equally honest reason: I did not believe that all those things in Genesis were true. When he told me I had to accept such things on faith, I decided I could never be a Christian.

The behavior of the lay members of a congregation can also create barriers. My father-in-law was one of the finest men I ever met, honest and kind. He was a responsible citizen, and he looked after his family. As members of the older generation became incapacitated by age and illness, he was the one who visited them in the hospital and tended to their affairs. He was everything I think a Christian ought to be, but after he left the home of his parents, he never again went to church.

The reason was, he told me, that soon after he entered the business world he discovered that some of the town's leading citizens and most outspoken Christians were dishonest. He could not attend church and participate in such hypocrisy.

I admit that the behavior of hypocritical Christians created a barrier for me until a theological school professor told our class, "Hypocrisy is the tribute vice pays to virtue." He pointed out that society was better off with hypocrites than it would be with business men who claimed that dishonesty and crooked dealing were virtuous forms of behavior. Hypocrisy at least helps society pass on a value system to the next generation, who may actually take the values more seriously than their parents.

One barrier that stands between skeptics and the church arises more in the present than in memories of past offenses: the possible disapproval of family and friends. Other skeptics may think that church-goers are soft in the head. They may also feel threatened when one of their number decides that there may be something of value in organized religion. They tend to react to this threat with defensive behavior, such as making sarcastic comments or avoiding the company of the defector.

Being made to feel odd or deficient by family and friends can be an unpleasant experience, but often such unpleasantness is more than balanced by welcome surprises. When fellow skeptics discover one of their number is investigating a church, some of them may quietly confess their envy of church people and may in some thinly disguised manner admit to their longing for God. Others may admire the courage of a fellow skeptic who has decided to pursue a long-repressed interest in Christianity.

Both the disapproval and the approval of family and friends can actually work to the advantage of a skeptic who is going to church. The disapproval is a reminder that all communities worthy of the name have boundaries. People have to know the difference between being out and being in for the belonging to have any significance. The approval may open the way to interesting conversation and new areas of intimacy. When two people admit that they have the same secret interest in religion, they often form a bond that strengthens them both as they pursue their quest for meaning.

As a rule skeptics are willing to make fair assessments of the barriers that confront them as they consider the possibility of church. They will see that most of the barriers are emotional, based upon unsatisfactory relationships with people unconnected to the Christian community that now interests them. By examining the experiences that have created the barriers, skeptics can usually put them in a perspective that allows them to move beyond the barriers to an exploration of what the church has to offer.

Intellectual barriers, however, present the skeptic with another kind of problem. The Bible, the Nicene Creed, and the business of prayer need thoughtful study. In order to maintain their intellectual integrity, skeptics are obliged to find ways of thinking about these things before professing themselves to be Christians. The following three chapters offer a way for skeptics to be honest with themselves and still accept what is basic to the practice of Christianity.

Chapter 3
THE BIBLE—A Reflection Of Human Existence

"You know, I've never really believed that Jonah swallowed a whale, or the whale swallowed Jonah, whichever way it was. I know we're supposed to believe what's in the Bible, but there are some things in the book that just don't make no sense to me so I try not to think about them and hope the good Lord won't hold it against me."

That was the way an elderly country woman in West Virginia described her approach to the Bible when she first joined a study group in her parish church. Like everyone else who wants to practice Christianity, she had to find some way of accommodating herself to the collection of ancient writings that are supposed to contain "all things necessary to salvation", as the Prayer Book so quaintly puts it. Born believers seldom have trouble with the Bible, since they can believe anything, but skeptical people usually find that parts of the Bible are difficult to accept.

Miracles

If you find some items of interest in the Bible but are put off by descriptions of events that seem highly improbable at best, you are in good company. I have on my bookshelf a copy of the New Testament edited by the third president of the United States, Thomas Jefferson. His version is much shorter than any other I have come across, the reason being that he has omitted every episode that smacks of the miraculous, including the resurrection of Jesus. Since miracles seem to create the most serious barrier to the reading of the Bible, miracles can provide a starting place for skeptics looking for an acceptable approach to this daunting book.

When people use the word "miracle", they are usually referring to an event or action that apparently contradicts known scientific laws. From the perspective of the twentieth century, the Bible describes many events and actions that fit this definition of miracle. The two most frequently cited by skeptics are

the people of Israel crossing the Red Sea and Jesus walking
on water:

> Then Moses stretched out his hand over the sea; and the
> Lord drove the sea back by a strong East wind all night, and
> made the sea dry land, and the waters were divided. And
> the people of Israel went into the midst of the sea on dry
> ground, the waters being a wall to them on their right hand
> and on their left. (Exodus 14:21-22)

> When evening came, his disciples went down to the sea, got
> into a boat, and started across the sea to Capernaum. It
> was now dark, and Jesus had not yet come to them. The
> sea rose because a strong wind was blowing. When they
> had rowed about three or four miles, they saw Jesus walk-
> ing on the sea and drawing near to the boat. They were
> frightened, but he said to them, "It is I; do not be afraid."
> Then they were glad to take him into the boat, and im-
> mediately the boat was on the land to which they were going.
> (John 6:16-21)

To the modern skeptic these two accounts cannot possibly
be descriptions of historical events because they contradict
known scientific laws. Drops of water cannot be piled up like
so many cinder blocks to form parallel walls along the sides of
a roadway, nor can a human body or any other object be placed
in water without sinking far enough to displace water equal to
its own weight. So how can a skeptic who wants to practice
Christianity come to terms with the miracles recorded in the
Bible? Three approaches, each offering at least a degree of
intellectual respectability, are available: ignoring, explaining,
or taking the stories literally. Although the first two are more
popular, I think the third offers the most promising approach,
surprising as it may seem at first glance. After briefly describing how the other two approaches work, I will explain in some
detail how taking the miracle stories literally can be done with
intellectual integrity.

Both Thomas Jefferson and the old country woman from
West Virginia found that ignoring the unacceptable stories
worked best for them. By simply setting aside the miracles
they were able to find wisdom and guidance in other parts of
the Bible. They found value in reading and studying it as long
as they did not trouble themselves over what seemed im-
plausible. I see nothing morally out of line with this approach;

in fact I read novels in the same manner. I often skim over the philosophical musings of the author because I find them offensive and because they throw me off the primary track of the story. If I refused to pick up any book containing right-wing political views, however, my supply of leisure reading material would be unnecessarily limited and my life would be impoverished. The same principle may hold true for the Bible. People who refuse to read it because they are offended by miracles deny themselves the possibility of enrichment from many other passages that contain no miraculous elements. Skimming over the miracles may be the best way to read the Bible for many skeptics.   Other skeptics try to find logical explanations for the events that appear in the Bible as miracles. For example, many people who are normally put off by miracles have been relieved to hear that the "Red Sea" crossed by the people of Israel, may in fact be a mistranslation for the "Sea of Reeds", a tidal estuary that may have been sufficiently dried by a strong wind during a low tide to allow the fugitives to escape. Then when the tide came rushing back with exceptional force, the Egyptians were trapped in the sea and drowned.

In a similar fashion, people have been able to accept the walking-on-water episode as an historical event in which the eyes of the disciples played a trick on them. They had been rowing for several miles in the dark during a storm and had assumed that they were far out toward the middle of the Sea of Galilee, when in fact they had been blown close to the shore. Jesus was simply walking along the beach when they caught sight of him emerging from the darkness. That explains why "immediately the boat was at the land" when Jesus got in. Using this approach skeptics can live with the miracles, knowing that behind each miracle story lies an explanation that fits with their understanding of the laws of nature. The challenge of finding such an explanation can be both stimulating and amusing for the skeptical reader of the Bible.

The third solution is to take the stories literally. If this suggestion shocks you, please pause to ponder the literal meaning of the word "literally". To take a passage literally is to read the words as the author intended them. To take a story literally is to uphold the meaning of the words in the context and in the language in which they were written. In his magnificent exposition on the Bible and literature, *The Great Code*, Northrop Frye insists that to take the Bible literally is to take each passage as written without imposing a post-seventeenth-century scientific world view upon the text. According to Frye, "Traditionally, the Bible's narrative has been regarded as 'literally' historical and its meaning as 'literally' doctrinal or didactic: the present book takes myth and metaphor to be the true literal bases."

All of the biblical stories, you must remember, were written long before the revolution in human thought and perception that came with the discovery of scientific principles in the seventeenth century. When the miracle stories in the Bible were written, the authors could not have been attempting to describe an event that contradicts the laws of nature, because they had no knowledge of such laws. Nor were they trying to write history as we know it, because attempts at recording facts to give an objective view of the past was an enterprise no one attempted until the seventeenth century. As Barbara Tuchman noted in her foreword to *A Distant Mirror*, an account of the fourteenth century:

> The chronic exaggeration of medieval numbers—of armies, for example—when accepted as factual, has led in the past to a misunderstanding of medieval war as analogous to modern war, which it was not, in means, method, or purpose. It should be assumed that medieval figures for military forces, battle casualties, plague deaths, revolutionary hordes, processions, or any groups en masse are generally enlarged by several hundred percent. This is because the chroniclers did not use numbers as data but as a device of literary art to amaze or appall the reader.

In much the same fashion, the miracle stories in the Bible were written not for a scientific or historic purpose but to convey a sense of amazement or wonder that would bond the reader more closely with the religious community. To take a miracle story literally, then, is to set aside all questions of "What really happened?" because what really happened was not on the author's mind. To take the story literally is to open yourself to the sense of awe and wonder that the author was trying to communicate. In telling the story about dividing the waters of the Red Sea, the author was probably using an incident known in the folklore of Israel to talk about the awesome experience of being set free from economic and political bondage through life in a community of faithful people. In telling the story about Jesus walking on the water, the author may well have been trying to communicate a personal experience of what it is like to be set free from fear when life seems out of control. What is central to both miracle stories is not what took place in the past, but the possibilities available to the reader for the future.

Unfortunately, the word "literally" has been badly distorted in recent years. When people talk about taking the Bible literally, what they mean is that they attribute to the biblical words contemporary meanings and intentions as if the authors were interested in facts and events.

Until relatively recent times if people had some important truths to communicate to other members of their community, they did so through the myths and metaphors that come naturally to poetic forms of speech and writing. The "life" of a saint written in the seventh century is much closer to the Biblical form of expression than it is to modern biography. To take only one example, in Adomnan's life of St. Columba, the abbot of Iona who brought Christianity from Ireland to Scotland, he told the truth about St. Columba's revered place in the community and about his contribution to the spread of Christianity through pagan lands by relating stories in classical, mythological forms. One of my favorites is the account of a spiritual duel between St. Columba and Broichan, the court druid in the household of Brude, king of the Picts. Having lost every contest, Broichan made one last attempt to get even by calling up a contrary wind when St. Columba was trying to leave the court of Brude and to sail back to Iona:

> So our Columba, seeing that the elements were being roused to fury against him, called upon Christ the Lord. He entered the boat, and while the sailors hesitated, he himself, more steadfast, ordered the sail to be raised against the wind. When this was done with the whole crowd looking on, the ship moved with extraordinary speed, sailing against the contrary wind.

Most of us living in the twentieth century have a hard time imagining what life was like before "truth" was made to equal "being in accordance with the facts". Until after the Reformation and the dawning of the Age of Reason, people communicated trivial truths by reporting the facts of everyday life, but they customarily conveyed significant truths through miracle stories, stories that used the poetic language of myth and metaphor to convey a sense of awe and wonder. Skeptical people might find their lives enriched if they could acquire such a sense of the miraculous in their own experience. The person who helped me the most in seeing miracles was Barry Block, a lonely young man in a class I helped lead. At a critical turning point in the life of the class, Barry wrote a song acknowledging the loneliness that had tormented him until he learned to listen to other people in the class and to be honest with them about himself. In the song he admitted that all his life he had "felt like a stranger, short on friendship and courage to care", but a change had taken place. The song comes to a conclusion with the refrain:

> And i find myself loving you
> and it's a Miracle Yes
> i find myself loving you
> and it's a Miracle

Skeptics may approach miracle stories that involve the healing of sick people in the same ways that they deal with nature miracles, but for me there is a difference. The healing miracles can be ignored and they can be taken literally, but I think that they can be explained in a more useful way than can the stories about the wind and the sea.

Ignoring the healing miracles in the Bible may be the best approach, especially for skeptics who have strong feelings about damage that may have been done to friends or members of their own families who were duped into seeking miraculous cures for life-threatening ailments. My father's best friend in high school was allowed to die of pneumonia without medical attention while the parents of the unfortunate boy prayed for a miracle. Anyone with that kind of experience is not likely to look with much favor on the stories that are used to persuade the gullible that they should refuse to accept the gifts of modern medicine.

Taking the healing stories literally is also a respectable option for non-believers. The gospels use healing miracles as a literary device. Take the tenth chapter of the Gospel according to St. Mark as an example. Mark pictures Jesus as particularly unsuccessful in conveying his vision of life to his disciples. They misunderstand his attitude toward children. They do not get what he is trying to tell them about appropriate attitudes toward possessions. He tells them that he will probably die in Jerusalem, and two of the disciples respond by asking for special places of honor in the new order that they assume is coming. After conveying this series of episodes that demonstrate the disciples' blindness to what Jesus was teaching them, Mark inserts a story about Jesus healing the blind beggar Bartimaeus. Clearly this healing story is to be taken as a metaphor; it anticipates the opening of the disciples' blind eyes after the death of Jesus.

Although ignoring the healing miracles or taking them literally may be the best approach for many skeptics, I think that many of the stories make sense. I came to that conclusion some years ago when reflecting on an article I had read by two physicians about the ways past ages and other cultures have dealt with illness—such as starving, leeching, purging, and engaging in rituals of purification or countersorcery. The authors claimed that a placebo, a treatment that has no bio-chemical basis but does provide reassurance to the patient, might be the best remedy for 60% to 80% of all medical complaints because these illnesses have an emotional rather than physiological cause. In addition, a placebo often proves to be therapeutic even with illnesses of a demonstrated biological origin. Following this line of argument, I can find no reason for supposing that Jesus did not heal people who came to him in the confidence that they could be healed and who submitted themselves to the ritual forms of treatment that Jesus used. I assume that in the first century, just as in the twentieth, approximately three-fourths of all illness had a psychological origin so that the healing methods of Jesus were medically appropriate. Furthermore, by making good use of the placebo effect Jesus could also have healed some people suffering from illnesses with a bio-chemical cause.

Although I think skeptics can gain more from their study of the Bible by taking the healing miracles literally, if stories of miraculous healing are also studied in the light of scientific medicine, they can provide the modern reader with useful insight into the healing of some illnesses.

Other Offensive Material

Miracles are not the only kinds of material that get in the way of skeptical people finding value in the Bible. Some skeptics have found that no matter where they open the Bible they are stymied by the language and form of the text. Every page seems to be written in an alien and incomprehensible style. Others, who have found the style to be acceptable if not altogether charming, have thought that they would give the Bible a try and have set out to read the whole thing from start to finish. They often do fairly well taking the Bible-as-literature approach to the King James Version until they come to "And unto Enoch was born Irad: and Irad begat Mehujael: and Mehujael begat Methusael . . ." After a few more begats they give up on the Old Testament and decide to start at the beginning of the New with the Gospel according to St. Matthew. And what do they find? "Abraham begat Isaac; and Isaac begat Jacob; and Jacob begat Judas . . ."

Other skeptics have plunged on into the Bible and have found themselves offended by the behavior of God. God sometimes appears to be arbitrary and cruel. He favors a sneak like Jacob over his honest but plodding brother, Esau. He encourages the people of Israel to occupy an already settled land and to destroy the original inhabitants. He allows a bear to devour little boys whose only offense was teasing a prophet. In the New Testament as well as the Old, God seems always ready to destroy the innocent in the process of punishing the wicked.

Skeptical women often have a special problem in reading the Bible. Most of the stories are about men, and even the few stories about women seem to be told from the male point of view. God appears to be masculine, and most of God's representatives are men, including the person most important to Christians, Jesus of Nazareth. Both the Hebrew Scriptures and the Gospels give the impression that the only reasonable organization of human beings is a patriarchal system.

Whenever I hear skeptics telling about how they have been put off by offensive passages in the Bible, I am reminded of Rabbi Bernard Mehlman's dictum: "No one should ever read the Bible. You should study the Bible, or leave it alone." When people try to read the Bible, they may be offended because they are unaware that it is not a book in the usual sense of the word. The Bible is a peculiar assortment of material accumulated from oral sources, written and edited over a period of at least twelve hundred years. To extract meaning from this odd collection of ancient writings, you need to study the texts carefully with whatever assistance you can find.

If you want to get past the offensive material in order to look for something of value in the Bible, you then decide what method to employ in Bible study. In looking for an acceptable method, skeptics may be surprised to learn that the way fundamentalists study the Bible is a fairly recent phenomenon. I was surprised, and pleased, to learn that studying the Bible to discover scientific and historical facts is a method that was not fully developed until 1895 at a Bible Conference of Conservative Protestants held in Niagara. Fundamentalism was a response to the critical method of Bible study, which had itself taken shape along with the development of science beginning in the eighteenth century. In the seventeen hundred years before the critical method was employed, however, Christians studied the Bible in much the same way that St. Paul had studied the Hebrew Scriptures.

How the Ancients Studied the Scriptures

St. Paul demonstrated his method of Bible study in writing his First Letter to the Christians at Corinth, with whom he was having some disagreements. The following excerpt comes from the tenth chapter:

> I want you to know, brethren, that our fathers were all under the cloud, and all passed through the sea, and all were baptized into Moses in the cloud and in the sea, and all ate the same supernatural food and all drank the same supernatural drink. For they drank from the supernatural Rock which followed them, and the Rock was Christ. Nevertheless with

most of them God was not pleased; for they were over-
thrown in the wilderness.

After summarizing the failures of Moses' followers and the
disasters that befell them, St. Paul then declares:

Now these things happened to them as a warning, but they
were written down for our instruction.

Two words in this brief statement require special attention
because the English translation does not quite convey Paul's
meaning. For "warning" St. Paul uses *tupos*, from which we
get our word "type". *Tupos* originally meant a blow from a
hammer or an ax; later it came to stand for the mark left by
the blow, such as a blaze pointing the way along a trail. The
second word, "instruction" comes from a Greek compound
word meaning "to put or place the mind". A paraphrase of
what St.Paul wrote might be, "Now these things happened in
the past as marks along the way that can help us develop an
appropriate mind set toward our own lives." No matter how
we choose to translate the sentence, the meaning seems fairly clear. St. Paul has studied the sacred writings of his people,
not to find out what really happened in the past, but to find
guidance for the future. The method he has used is called
"allegory170. He has found a story that in some ways seems
to parallel his present situation and has retold the story to
provide insight that he thinks will be helpful to the Christian
community in Corinth.

In writing to the Christians in Galatia, St. Paul is quite explicit about using the allegorical method:

Tell me, you who desire to be under law, do you not hear
the law? For it is written that Abraham had two sons, one
by a slave and one by a free woman. But the son of the
slave was born according to the flesh, the son of the free
woman through promise. Now this is an allegory: these
women are two covenants. St. Paul uses the allegory to
make his claim that Christians should think of themselves as
free-born people, like the children of Abraham's wife Sarah,
and not as people under bondage, like the children of the
slave woman, Hagar. Once again, we see that apparently
St. Paul was not particularly interested in what really happened; instead, he is looking for guidance. If you had asked
him, "Do you think that the story about Abraham and Sarah
and Hagar really happened?" he would probably have

replied, "I suppose so, but why do you ask? O Such a question would not have occurred to him.

Although St. Paul would probably have been astounded to think that his hastily written letters might themselves some day be regarded as Holy Scripture, he would probably not have been surprised to learn that his method of Bible study would endure through the middle ages. Northrop Frye quotes Dante to demonstrate the medieval method of Bible study:

> To elucidate, then, what we have to say, be it known that the sense of this work is not simple, but on the contrary it may be called polysemous, that is to say, "of more senses than one"; for it is one sense which we get through the letter, and another through the thing the letter signifies; and the first is called literal, but the second is allegorical or mystic.

Dante was not presenting a new approach, but simply repeating what all learned Christians knew to be true. They studied the Bible to find analogies with their own lives that would provide them with theological insight, moral guidance, and *anagoge*, that is, a "leading upwards" or a "spiritual uplift".

Analogy was the only accepted method of Bible study until the eighteenth century, when the spirit of scientific inquiry began to affect the way Christian scholars studied the Bible and led them to use the newer critical methods. They developed a curiosity about the culture of the people who produced various parts of the Bible, incorporating into their study of the Bible the latest findings in the fields of archaeology, geography, and cultural anthropology. Such scholars took delight in mastering the ancient languages in which the Bible was written, Hebrew and Greek, as well as the Aramaic spoken by Jesus and the Syriac employed in one of the first translations of the Bible.

These scholars discovered that the Bible did not suddenly appear as a completed book but included two collections of material that did not reach their present shape until dates that are surprisingly late. The rabbis did not decide until ninety years after the birth of Jesus what would be the sacred texts of the Jewish people. This collection of Hebrew Scripture, which Christians call the Old Testament, excluded many documents that had been included in some previous collections. The most notable of the earlier versions of the Hebrew Scriptures is the "Septuagint", a Greek translation that was produced in Alexandria two centuries before the Christian era. The books in the Septuagint that the rabbis ultimately rejected were revered by many early Christians for whom the Greek version of the Hebrew Scriptures was the only Bible they had known. These books appeared in the first Latin translations of the Bible and are still accepted as holy scripture by Roman Catholics. Among Protestants these rejected parts of the Septuagint have a more ambiguous status and are called the "Apocrypha", meaning "that which was hidden away".

Christians took a long time to agree on which of their early writings would be revered as sacred literature. Lists of gospels and letters began appearing in the second century but the matter was not settled until the beginning of the fifth century. By that time numerous gospels had made their appearance, but only four were included in what came to be called the New Testament. Many Christians thought that the letters of Clement, one of the first bishops of Rome, should be in the collection, but they were finally left out because he had not been an apostle. At the same time, some letters were accepted because people thought they had been written by St. Paul, such as First and Second Timothy; we now know that these letters reflect conditions long after Paul's time. Many of the early lists of sacred Christian writings omit the last book that finally achieved acceptance, Revelation. Over the ages, many Christians have thought that the inclusion of the book of Revelation in the New Testament was a great mistake and has done more harm than good.

The Critical Method

As Christian scholars developed an appreciation for the Bible as a collection of documents gathered from a culture quite remote from their own, they developed tools for a critical approach to the study of the scriptures. Among the methods that they began to use in the eighteenth century and that their successors use today are form criticism, redaction criticism, and textual criticism.

Scholars have noted that certain identifiable types of stories appear in the Bible as well as in other ancient literature. A story of a certain type or "form" in the Bible usually has much in common with similar stories from other traditions, such as explanations for place names or for natural phenomena like the rainbow. By comparing similar stories, scholars learned how ancient writers took episodes from the lore embodied in the oral tradition of their people and retold the story to make a new point. For example, the flood story told in Genesis chapters six through nine is very similar to the flood stories of other cultures, but it seems to make a different point. The original story may have been about mortality, but the present version in the Bible is about the relationship between God and human beings.

Form criticism has also helped scholars to uncover the original meanings of the parables and the miracles in the New Testament that had been lost over the centuries in which Christians had studied the stories only for the purpose of finding analogies with their own situations. Form criticism has helped to separate what might have been the original intent of Bible stories from the use later generations have made of them.

What scholars call "redaction" criticism is a based on a process the rest of us refer to as "cut and paste" editing. Anyone with a critical eye can see that the first three chapters of Genesis are not the work of one author but are composed of two separate stories that have been pasted together. Genesis 1:1 - 2:3 is written in a completely different style from 2:4 - 3:25. The two stories also differ in substance at several critical points as they tell the story of creation. The first story accounts for the creation of all other living things before the appearance of human beings. In the second story, the human creature appears first, then the plants, and then the animals. In the first story, human beings are created male and female. In the second, the human creature, who appears first on the scene before all other living things, is not sexually differentiated until later. The pasting together of these two stories is obviously the work of an editor who was more interested in preserving the lore of the Jewish people than in putting together a logical or consistent history. Using the techniques of redaction criticism, scholars study the editing of ancient material to see how these stories were put together over the years until they achieved their present form.

Redaction criticism has also opened up new avenues for the study of the New Testament. Seeing the gospels as the work of creative editors helped scholars to explain both the similarities and the differences among the four accounts of the life and teaching of Jesus. By comparing the gospels, they could see that Matthew, Mark, and Luke used some of the same sources while John worked from an independent tradition. As they looked more closely at the three similar gospels, they discovered that most of Mark is included in both Matthew and Luke, in many places almost word for word. The most popular theory is that Matthew and Luke used Mark as one source and that they had another source in common, a collection of Jesus' teaching. Matthew and Luke then appended other material from their own special sources in the oral tradition, such as the stories of Jesus' birth. To see the composers of the gospels as editors rather than authors allows a student of the Bible to appreciate the way each handled the material to put across a particular point of view.

Textual criticism is based on the fact that no book of the Bible is available in a first edition. No original manuscript for any portion of either the Hebrew Scriptures or the New Testament of the Christians exists today. Scholars who want to find out what the original editors actually wrote must work from copies of copies, so whenever they locate an ancient copy of a book in the Bible, they compare it to the texts that they have studied previously. In making these comparisons they inevitably find differences, because the scribes who made the copies were all too human. Sometimes a different reading is obviously the result of a mistake, such as a line repeated or dropped, or a sentence that makes no logical or grammatical sense. Sometimes a scribe apparently added an editorial comment or explanation of his own or inserted a phrase he picked up from somewhere else in the Bible. Some scribes tried to correct the text, while others tried to remove embarrassing contradictions.

Most of the differences among the available ancient copies of biblical material do not affect the meaning of specific passages, but occasionally one of these variations becomes quite important for people trying to understand the original intent of an editor or writer. For example, in closing his letter to the Christians in Rome, St. Paul included this greeting:

> Greet Andronicas and Junias, my kinsmen and my fellow prisoners; they are men of note among the apostles, and they were in Christ before me. (Romans 16:7)

The problem is that the name "Junias" in some manuscripts appears as "Junia" in others. The dispute over the masculine and feminine forms was critical in the debate concerning the ordination of women in the Episcopal Church because Paul had identified this person as an apostle, like himself. Translators have disguised the possible ambiguity in English versions of the verse by calling relatives "kinsmen" and by causing an adjective meaning "outstanding" to read "men of note". Many textual critics assume that some ancient scribes probably had the same bias as modern English translators who insist on inserting the word "men" into the text. These critics have a rule: when in doubt, take the more difficult reading, the one that runs counter to prevailing values and ways of thinking. Following this rule, textual criticism suggests that one of the few people St. Paul honored with the title apostle was indeed a woman.

The Fundamentalist Response

The new critical approach to the Bible upset some Christians in the nineteenth century, by and large the same Christians who were also distressed by the new discoveries in several rapidly developing fields of science, particularly geology, astronomy, and biology. Many of these discoveries seemed to contradict what they read in the Bible, the foundation of their faith. If what the Bible says is true, then what the scientists were saying about the age of the world and the evolution of living creatures must be wrong. To preserve their faith, such Christians rejected both the findings of modern science and the use of critical methods in the study of the Bible.

The anti-scientific movement in the church gradually gained momentum in the late nineteenth century and in 1911 acquired a name, "fundamentalism", from a series of twelve tracts entitled *The Fundamentals*, produced in the United States and distributed throughout the English speaking world with the aid of American money. Although the fundamentalists saw scientists as their enemy, they failed to notice that in their protest they had abandoned basic principles of religion and had adopted the values of their adversaries. Just as CIA agents in trying to protect democracy sometimes start thinking and acting like the terrorists they are trying to thwart, the fundamentalists took on a "scientific" way of equating truth with what is historically and objectively factual. They gave up the religious understanding of truth as insights which lead us ever more deeply into the mystery of our lives and of God. Instead of looking to the Bible for knowledge of their relationship with God, moral guidance, and spiritual uplift—as Dante and countless other Christians over the centuries had done—they expected the Bible to provide them with facts about the origin of the universe and facts about human history.

Once the fundamentalists had accepted the scientific meaning of truth, they could no longer take the Bible literally. That is, they could no longer read the Bible in the way that the original authors had intended it to be read. What the Bible editors had presented as myth and metaphor, offered to illuminate the relationship between human beings and God, the fundamentalists read as if the material came from a journal of science or history. Having taken the position that the Bible was factually accurate in all respects, they were forced to invent explanations for all of the obvious contradictions between passages in the Bible and between the Bible and scientific data. For example, they have accepted the calculations of a seventeenth-century archbishop of Armagh who counted the number of generations mentioned in Genesis and decided that the world was created in 4004 B.C. How then do they account for the discovery of dinosaur fossils that appear to be millions of years old? They say that bones were planted by the devil to undermine the people's faith in the Bible.

The point is that fundamentalism is a modern phenomenon without roots in the Christian tradition. The tragedy is that fundamentalists have convinced many skeptics that fundamentalism is the only legitimate approach to Christianity. The irony is that, just as fundamentalists bought the scientific view of truth, so numerous skeptics have allowed the fundamentalists to set the terms on which the Bible must be studied and judged.

Many skeptics are taken aback when they learn that the fundamentalists' approach to the Bible is unacceptable to most educated Christians. A skeptic's response to hearing about the critical method of studying the Bible might be: "I know that Christians are supposed to believe that the Bible has no factual errors, and I have read enough of the Bible to know that such a belief is ridiculous. Therefore, I have known for a long time that I can never be a Christian and that I can never take the Bible seriously. Now you people come along and tell me that educated and intelligent Christians find meaning in the Bible that has nothing to do with factual accuracy, and I start doubting the basis of my position as a non- Christian. I start wondering if the Bible and the church might have something of value for me, and then I find myself with an internal conflict over religion, a conflict I thought I had laid to rest long ago." Some skeptical people, in order to re-assure themselves that they did the right thing by rejecting Christianity, insist that the fundamentalist approach to the Bible is the only correct point of view for Christians.

The Bible as a Mirror of Human Experience

Once people are willing to set aside the pseudo-scientific notions of fundamentalism, they are free to explore the Bible as the product of religious communities drawing on the lore of their people as they struggle to make sense out of their existence. The point of studying the Bible is that the effort of ancient people to find meaning in the mysteries of life and death may illuminate our search for answers to the eternal, unanswerable questions.

Anyone who decides to study the Bible must settle on an approach to the subject. One approach that has worked well for many naturally skeptical people is to accept Holy Scripture as historical fiction. Most people are familiar with historical fiction as a literary form. When they attend a production of Shakespeare's Julius Caesar, they know perfectly well that Mark Antony's oration over Caesar's body is an invention of the playwright. They know that while the characters in the play may represent actual historical figures, they also realize that the plot is loosely based on Shakespeare's limited knowledge of historical events and that he made up all of the dialogue. That the play is largely fiction, however, does not detract from its power or its value. People have responded to the play, not because it is good history, but because they can see themselves in the conflicts of loyalty and in the quests for power that the actors project.

People can learn to approach the Bible in the same way. Many of the stories are loosely based on the lives of people who may have been historical figures, such as Abraham and Moses. Jesus of Nazareth was almost certainly a real person. All of the words and actions attributed to them, however, are the work of creative authors with little to go on but what the bearers of the oral tradition remembered of what they themselves had been told. From the raw material of folklore, the biblical writers and editors created ways of preserving their insights for the guidance of future generations. The form many of them chose was what we today call historical fiction.

Actually, the form some of the biblical authors chose was pure fiction, with little attempt at making a historical connection. The book about Jonah was certainly made up simply to challenge some of the chauvinistic attitudes that had emerged among the people of Judah after the exile.

Most of the stories, however, do have some historical connection—but that is not the point. History buffs may find in the Bible some useful clues about ancient events if they are willing to weigh the evidence carefully against other sources of information, but the real value of Bible study will not emerge if people are primarily trying to figure out what really happened. The truths of fiction, either of the pure or historical type, do not emerge from the facts but from glimpses into the mystery of human experience.

To get the most from Bible study, the serious student must bring specific questions to the text. I have found three questions that always seem to be useful: For whom was the passage originally written? What was the author or editor telling them? What does the passage suggest to us?

Getting answers to the first two questions requires some work. To find what kind of people were originally being addressed and to uncover the meanings of the original words and phrases, a Bible student has to read the work of the scholars who have devoted their lives to such questions. Of course, it is possible to read the Bible without such research, but then Bible study becomes merely a verbal Rorschach test. Letting the biblical images evoke feelings and stir up memories can be immensely valuable to someone seeking self-awareness, but such an approach may miss the wisdom of the author or editor. Such an approach also usually avoids any challenge to customary ways of thinking and any judgment on conventional ways of behaving. To gain access to the best a passage has to offer, a student of the Bible has to do the necessary homework.

1. For whom was the passage originally written?

This question helps get at the meaning of the text in two ways. On the one hand, the more we know about the culture and the concerns of the intended audience, the more likely we will be to catch the implications of the words. On the other hand, the text itself will reveal more about the culture and concerns of the audience than it will about the events it records. That is true about the literature of any age. For example, Gibbon's *Decline and Fall of the Roman Empire* tells us more about eighteenth-century England than it does about ancient Rome; to understand the book you have to have some knowledge of English imperialism.

The question about the audience is more complicated when dealing with the Bible, however, for in reading the Bible we often have to deal with more than one audience. The Gospel according to St. Luke, for example, indicates the presence of at least three different audiences in the process of its development.

In its present form, the gospel is addressed to the "most excellent Theophilus". The intended readers were either a high official in the Roman empire and his household, or else were people in the Roman aristocracy who could identify with such an official, whether he were a real person or a symbolic "lover of God", which is what his name means. The form of address, the Greek language in which it is written, and other internal evidence all point to an educated Gentile audience living in a metropolitan area far from Palestine during the latter part of the first century, at least forty years after the death of Jesus.

Yet the original sources for Luke's material could not have been Gentiles nor could their language have been Greek nor their culture urban. That material originally came from the Aramaic-speaking Palestinian peasants who formed the first Christian community following the death of Jesus. As far as we know—because Jesus had no scribes or secretaries following him around and recording his words and deeds—all Luke had to work from was what these followers of Jesus remembered and what they saw fit to tell the people who joined their community. The recent converts to Christianity in the generation following Jesus' death formed an audience prior to the one addressed by Luke, but still not the earliest one. The first audience, the disciples of Jesus, did not tell the new converts everything they remembered; they told the new members of their community what they thought they needed to know.

The first audience, whose culture and concerns are basic to an understanding of the gospel, was made up of the people to whom Jesus actually spoke. His words were filtered through the memories of his disciples, shaped to fit the needs of the first Christian community, and revised to win the respect of the Roman aristocracy—but in the gospels we can still find evidence of the fears and longings of the Palestinian peasants who constituted the first audience for the teaching of Jesus.

2. What was the author or editor telling them?

Returning to the Gospel according to St. Luke, we would ask: What was Luke's message for the Gentiles of the ruling class in the Roman empire? What did the disciples of Jesus want to teach those who joined their community? What was Jesus trying to convey to those who followed him?

Although we can never answer these questions with finality, we can increase our chances of getting closer to the truth by using the best that the Bible critics have produced. Many good commentaries on the gospels are available. They compare the way Luke handles material with the way it is used in the other gospels. They decipher difficult words. They provide alternate readings for passages that are not the same in all of the ancient texts. They can often show when the concerns of the three different communities have affected the form in which a passage now appears. Anyone who seriously wants to understand the Bible will need either to consult commentaries or to study with someone who has done so.

For example, Kenneth F. Bailey in his excellent commentary on the parables in the Gospel according to St. Luke has illuminated the exchange between Jesus and a follower found in Luke 9:59-60:

> To another he said, "Follow me." But he said, "Lord, let me first go and bury my father." But he said to him, "Leave the dead to bury their own dead; but as for you, go and proclaim the kingdom of God."

Luke's aristocratic Gentile audience would be likely to see in this passage a suggestion that to be a follower of Jesus might bring them into conflict with their social responsibilities, such as seeing to the proper burial of their parents at a time when the church might need them elsewhere. The first converts to Christianity following the death of Jesus, however, heard in these words a more radical demand on their loyalty. When Palestinian peasants spoke of a responsibility to "bury my father70, they were describing an obligation to remain at home and look after their parents until the parents died. If they accepted a call to proclaim the kingdom after the fashion of the new Christian community, they would have to abandon their families and become disobedient sons and daughters. The followers of Jesus who first heard words like these from Jesus must have been shocked and perplexed. Filial duty was the very foundation of Palestinian peasant society. How could their teacher even suggest the possibility of such disobedience? They no doubt remembered these words because they were so troubling.

3. What does the passage suggest to us?

If we look into this passage as if it were a mirror, dusted and polished by our work on the two prior questions, what might we see of ourselves? With this question we come to the point of Bible study. The Bible is useful only as it enables us to understand ourselves so that we can function more effectively in the world.

Looking at these few lines from Luke, we each will see something different depending on our experiences and our current situations. The first thing that comes to my mind is the eternal conflict I experience between the demands of the church for which I work and the needs of my immediate family. On further looking, however, I become aware of the claim my own father had upon me. He was one who espoused the philosophy: "It is better to be a big frog in a little puddle than a little frog in big puddle.70 I was nearly fifty years old before I discovered that I had developed a fear of success, somehow twisting his words to mean that I would lose his respect and love if I should become successful in a larger arena than the one in which he lived his life. My devotion to my father, even long after he was dead, kept me from being all that I could be. The radical nature of Jesus' words remind me that filial duty can block me from being what God intended. That does not mean that devotion to my parents and their welfare is wrong, but that such devotion must always be experienced in tension with whatever I was intended to be.

Once skeptical people can get past the barriers to the Bible, a wonderful new experience awaits. Study of the Bible can provide a way to what most people long for: a sense of continuity with the past, identification with a community, assistance in the search for meaning, and guidance in the exploration of the mysteries presented by life and death. The Bible can show the way to truth—not accurate scientific and historical facts—but the truth about human beings and their relationship to God.

Chapter 4
THE NICENE CREED—An Expression Of
Human Longing

When some skeptical people wander into a celebration of Holy Communion in an Episcopal church, they find the proceedings for the most part not altogether unpleasant. They may enjoy the music and the pageantry and find something of interest in the sermon. They can sing the hymns, and when they can find the appropriate place in the prayer book, they can even join in some of the responses made by the congregation. The language in most of the service seems like poetry, so they do not worry much about the meaning of the words. If anything at all in the worship causes them trouble, it is likely to be the recitation of the Nicene Creed.

When they get to the words "I believe" or "We believe", some skeptics become mute. Others gamely try to join in, only to discover that they choke on some of the words or phrases. The creed may be the most difficult barrier to participation in worship that some skeptics have to cross.

The barrier presented by the Nicene Creed may not be insurmountable, however, for skeptics who understand the origin of the word "creed". As I explained earlier, we call the statement a creed because its first word in Latin is CReDo, a verb based on the noun CaRDia, which means "heart". Because heart has no verb form in English, and because the literal translation "I place my heart" seemed wordy and awkward, credo turned up in English as "I believe in". "I believe in" had a clearly different meaning from the similar phrase, "I believe that", which translated the Latin opinor. Credo, "I believe in", means to have trust or confidence. Opinor, "I believe that", means to hold an intellectual proposition that may or may not be in accord with the facts.

If a person reciting the creed takes it as an expression of the heart, the words may accurately reflect a longing for one who is worthy of confidence and trust. The creed is not a series of propositions that the congregation claims to hold as a description of God. Any statement about God is bound to be both inaccurate and incomplete. If by reciting the creed the members of a congregation were saying they believed that God is a father, they would be setting themselves up to be proved wrong. For all we know, God may be a mother, or God may not exist in any way analogous to human experience. In reciting the creed, the congregation is not claiming to know the unknowable about God, but instead stating what everyone can know for certain, a longing for God that the images and metaphors of the creed put into manageable perspective.

Churches that sing instead of say the Nicene Creed may be wise. Set to music, the creed seems more obviously to be an expression of the heart rather than of the intellect. Still, understanding the meaning of *credo* frees skeptical people to read the words as poetry and to open themselves to new insights about their hunger for reassurance and for meaning. Once they remove the creed from the realm of logic, it may become a mirror reflecting back to them their longings and desires. When that happens, they can either say or sing the Nicene Creed with a clear conscience and genuine feeling.

The Book of Common Prayer provides two English translations of the Nicene Creed, one that dates back to the sixteenth century and one that is of more recent origin. Both are attempts to put into English a statement originally formulated in Greek and Latin at a council of Christian bishops and theologians called by the Emperor Constantine in the year 325. The more recent translation follows an ancient tradition of putting the creed in the first person plural to emphasize the words as an expression of what the community as a whole believes in rather than as a statement accurately representing the views of any particular individual. The "we believe in" form makes it easier for some skeptics to join in because they do not feel they are making a personal affirmation. In the more recent translation the Nicene Creed begins:

> We believe in one God,
> the Father, the Almighty,
> maker of heaven and earth,
> of all that is, seen and unseen.

Before skeptics find the Nicene Creed to be a useful reflection of the longing in their hearts, they will have to work through some of the obvious difficulties, beginning with God being pictured as "Father". Nobody has had perfect parents. Some parents were sufficiently adequate, however, to instill in the hearts of their children the notion that a perfect parent could always make them feel safe and loved. A perfect parent would nurture them toward maturity and independence but would always be available to comfort and restore them when they were bruised by the battles of life. No matter how self-sufficient people become, they experience times when they need to be utterly dependent long enough to find healing and to renew their strength.

Some people have terrible parents. One woman had an alcoholic father who abused her more than once when he was on a drunken rampage. Even worse, she could not recall ever being able to please him or to win from him a word of praise. When she brought home the news that she was graduating first in her class, her father had no reaction. As a result, the first several times she came to church as a skeptical adult, she had difficulty picturing her longing for God as a longing for a father. She tried switching the parental image to a female one, but that did not help. What came to her mind was the memory of her own whining, nagging, constantly complaining mother. Eventually she discovered that what had drawn her back to church was a longing for the parents she never had, the parents her natural mother and father could never be. Her desire for God was for a father and a mother who would protect her and affirm her worth as a person.

Calling God "the Almighty" also disturbs some people. They find comfort in picturing God as limited and helpless. That way they do not have to acknowledge their anger toward God when things go wrong, and they have a handy explanation for God's failure to act on their behalf. As long as we cannot know anything about God for sure, however, I would rather imagine God to be genuinely god-like, to have unlimited power. I would rather join such giants of faith as Abraham and Jeremiah in blaming an omnipotent God when things go wrong than I would make excuses for a puny deity.

Another way to acknowledge the power of God is to call God the "maker of heaven and earth". Astronomers reported in late 1986 their fascination with galaxy 3C326.1, which is twelve billion light years away from the earth. Sun-size stars had been forming in this remote galaxy at the rate of three thousand to five thousand a year. When I read about a place in the universe so far away that it takes light from there twelve billion years to reach the earth, I am filled with awe and wonder.

All people, skeptics included, have to ask themselves when they look at the stars if the universe was produced by a series of improbable accidents or by the mighty acts of God. Some investigators of natural history are content with trying to explain the complexity of the accidents. Others, like Albert Einstein, see themselves as knocking on heaven's door "to know what was in God's mind".

Since we cannot know for certain if the natural order is the result of chance or providence, we can choose how we want to think about the earth and the heavens. If we opt for providence, we are expressing our desire for the universe to make sense even though creation will always be a mystery to us.

In the Nicene Creed, as we confess our longing for the universe to make sense, we are also expressing our eagerness for the power we encounter in Jesus of Nazareth to be the same force that forms the stars and holds the planets in their courses. So it is that the metaphor now shifts from God as parent to God as child, from father to son:

We believe in one Lord, Jesus Christ,
the only Son of God,
eternally begotten of the Father,
God from God, Light from Light,
true God from true God,
begotten, not made,
of one being with the Father.
Through him all things were made.

To say the creed with integrity as a skeptical person, I must have decided that the focus of my longing for God will be Jesus of Nazareth. Apparently some of the people who knew Jesus in his wanderings through Judea and Galilee thought that in his presence they had been in the presence of God. They told stories about Jesus and passed on what they had learned from him to other people, who in turn began writing these things down. These writings—the letters of St. Paul, the four gospels, and the other documents in the collection we call the New Testament—are the primary sources of our knowledge about Jesus and his teaching. Although I know much wisdom can be gained through other sources, by joining in the creed I am saying that I have decided to direct my energy to discovering what I can find about my relationship to God, the universe, and myself through this person whose name was Jesus.

The name Jesus is the Greek form of the ancient Hebrew name Joshua. The name means "God helps" or "God saves" - Although it was a fairly common name when Jesus of Nazareth received it, his followers found it to be especially appropriate.

At some point in his public life, the followers of Jesus suggested that he must be the long-expected messiah. *Messiah* is a Hebrew word meaning "one anointed with oil". The Greek *christos*, or christ, is a literal translation of the Hebrew. When they called Jesus the Christ, they were saying that God had anointed him to be God's special representative on the earth. When the people of Judea talked about a new messiah, however, they had in mind someone like David, the king who united twelve quarrelsome tribes into a functioning nation. The messiah would drive out the Roman army of occupation and free the people of Israel from foreign domination. The messiah would re-establish the kingdom of David.

Jesus was not the kind of messiah most people looked for. He brought a different kind of freedom, freedom that was not political but personal. He set people free to face what they could not face, to obtain self understanding, and to receive a new way and a new life.

A story in the fourth chapter of the Gospel according to St. John describes the experience of a Samaritan woman who discovers that Jesus is the Christ for her. In this story Jesus sits by a well to rest and asks the woman of Samaria to give him a drink. She expresses surprise that a Jew would ask a Samaritan for a drink, since the two related tribes have refused to have anything to do with each other for generations. Jesus responds by saying, "If you knew the gift of God, and who it is saying to you, 'Give me a drink,' you would have asked him, and he would have given you living water." That was step one, helping her to recognize what she had been unwilling to acknowledge before: she was dissatisfied with her life, and she was thirsty for something more. Later in the conversation Jesus tells her to call her husband. When she admits that she has no husband, Jesus says that she is right in admitting she has no husband, "for you have had five husbands, and he whom you now have is not your husband." That was step two, giving her the possibility of seeing the kind of person she had become. Far from getting upset when Jesus confronted her with her own behavior, the woman rushes into her village and urges everyone, "Come see a man who told me all that I ever did." Her eagerness and excitement reveal that she has found a new and honest way of thinking about herself and a new way of dealing with the reality of her situation. She has reached step three. When she asks aloud, "Can this be the Christ?" the reader knows that she has received the possibility of finding a new life for herself.

When we call Jesus "the Christ" in reciting the creed, we are acknowledging a desire for a similar kind of freedom. We need help in facing the terrifying and painful reality of our own existence. We need help in becoming honest about the kind of people we really are. We need help in finding a new direction for our lives. When we know that we need direction, the phrases "one Lord" and "the only Son of God" may take on new meaning.

Some years ago, when I was fascinated by the forms of Christianity that had developed in the East, I had the good fortune to spend several hours in the company of G. E. H. Palmer, the translator of the *Philokalia*, a collection of writings attributed to the Eastern church fathers from the fourth to the fourteenth century. After I had explained my interest in the Orthodox Christianity that he had embraced, Mr. Palmer asked if I had ever heard the expression, "Many paths lead to the top of the mountain." After I eagerly assured him that I was acquainted with the statement, he went on to inquire if I had also heard that "a person who keeps changing paths is not likely ever to reach the top."

When I profess my confidence in "one Lord, Jesus Christ, the only Son of God", I am declaring that in my quest for meaning I will follow one path into the mystery. To embrace Christianity is not to deny the validity of any other religious tradition. It is to claim one tradition as my own.

The importance of access to the mystery of life and death is underscored by the phrases "eternally begotten" and "through whom all things were made". If experience of the Christ were limited to the man Jesus of Nazareth, then only first-century Palestinians would have had the possibility of receiving the freedom to face what they could not face, to obtain self-understanding, and to receive a new way and a new life. By declaring that Jesus in the role of Christ is "eternally begotten", we are declaring that all people everywhere in all times have the possibility of discovering the freedom that a few fortunate people found in a direct encounter with Jesus of Nazareth in a remote corner of the Roman Empire two thousand years ago. By saying that "all things were made" through the Christ, we are recalling the experience of first-century Jews who felt when they were with Jesus of Nazareth that they were in the presence of the Lord God of Israel, the creator of heaven and earth, whom their people had always worshiped and whom we may worship still.

The experience of God that Christians identify with Jesus, other people in other cultures identify by other names, but what happens to them is much like what happened to the woman of Samaria who met Jesus by the well. Look at the ancient Hebrew scriptures. Abraham the patriarch probably called God "Yah170, but he received the same capacity to face the constricted reality of his life and to find a new way as did the Samaritan woman. So did Ruth the Moabite woman and ancestor of King David, who worshiped her own tribal gods. When we talk about the experience of God as Son being inseparable from the experience of God as Father, we are using a mythological form that suggests universal access to the mystery of creation and to the capacity for personal awareness and change.

Having identified one aspect of God with Jesus of Nazareth, the Nicene Creed continues with a symbolic reflection based on his birth and death. At this point in the recitation of the creed, skeptics need to remember that what the congregation recites is not primarily history but rather what anthropologists call the "organizing myth" of the church:

> For us and for our salvation
> he came down from heaven:
> by the power of the Holy Spirit
> he became incarnate from the Virgin Mary,
> and was made man.
> For our sake he was crucified under Pontius Pilate;
> he suffered death and was buried.

"Salvation" was originally a military metaphor. It meant to be delivered from the hands of the enemy. For the metaphor to make sense in situations outside of combat zones, we need to know from what we want to be saved.

Curiously enough, most adults who show up at church do so, not when they are most in need of deliverance, but a year or so after surviving a threatening experience. When Sam first appeared at church, most of the people who met him would have described him as attractive, self-confident, and successful. He served on the staff of a Senate committee and was obviously admired by all his colleagues. After we got to know Sam, we learned that only two years earlier he had lost his job with a small consulting firm, and his wife had left him. He knew that he had to put his life back together, but at times he had been almost paralyzed by his guilt, anxiety, and despair. He had felt guilt over his failure as a provider and his failure to keep his wife's affection. He had been anxious about both his personal and professional future. On his worst days he had held little hope that his life would ever be better. Then almost without warning, one of his many contacts paid off; the chief counsel of a Senate committee offered him a position if he could start to work immediately. With employment came a return of his confidence in himself and his future; with confidence, the capacity to reflect on the trauma he had survived. In some strange way he felt something had been supporting him throughout this terrible period of his life, delivering him from the worst ravages that guilt, anxiety, and despair could inflict on a human being. Although it was some time before he could use the term comfortably, he had experienced salvation and had come to church looking for a way to acknowledge that he had been saved. He knew that his salvation lay not in the offer of a job, but in his survival until the job was offered.

Some Christians equate salvation with going to heaven when they die. For other followers of Jesus "heaven" is a metaphor representing the realm of God, the location of ultimate meaning as well as of ultimate mystery. Christians inherited the image of God's dwelling in the sky from the Jews. In their earliest experiences about which we know anything at all, the ancient Hebrew-speaking people encountered God on the tops of mountains or pictured God riding on the thunder clouds overhead. God dwelt on high, but in his mercy he would come down to visit his people when they called upon him. Using this mythological image, early Christians quite naturally spoke of the Son coming down from heaven.

Although the heaven metaphor employed to identify experiences of God has the sanction of long usage, the image has caused problems for many modern skeptics. Some of the problems have arisen with the heavens becoming a place of investigation and exploration in the dawning space age. Other problems have been around longer, such as identifying heaven as a place for people who have died. All of the problems exist, however, because of the tendency to treat heaven as if it were a place instead of a symbol. When skeptics remember to approach heaven as a symbolic word suggesting the realm of God, they often find that the ancient metaphor regains its usefulness.

Another symbolic expression that requires some effort from skeptics before they find it useful is the phrase "became incarnate from the Virgin Mary". This designation for the mother of Jesus points in two directions at the same time: Jesus was born as a human being, and Jesus was an extraordinary person.

The Council of Nicaea opposed the view expressed by some Christians that Jesus was pure spirit and only appeared to be human, as well as the view that Jesus was just an ordinary human being. To point to the mythological paradox of Jesus being both fully human and completely God, they included in the creed a reference to the stories of a fabulous birth found in the gospels according to Matthew and Luke.

A close reading of the birth narratives in both Matthew and Luke, however, reveal that the authors knew they were using the language of myth, writing not history but theology. Matthew and Luke are the only New Testament authors who make any reference to the birth of Jesus or suggest that his mother was a virgin. Even they agree only on the place of the birth, the names of Jesus' parents, and their delay of sexual intercourse until after his birth. Besides relating stories about Jesus' birth, these two gospels also provide genealogies of Jesus tracing his ancestry through Joseph. (See Matthew 1:1-16 and Luke 3:23-38.) We have to assume that the authors of the gospels could not have failed to notice the contradiction between the birth stories and the genealogies. Had they been attempting to write an accurate history, the contradiction would make no sense. Because they were writing gospels, it made perfect sense for them to use a mythological birth story to reflect the impact Jesus had made on their lives and to use a genealogy to show that in their minds Jesus was the heir to David's kingdom.

Both birth stories seem to have been influenced by the verse from Isaiah quoted by Matthew (1:23): "a virgin shall conceive and bear a son." This quotation, taken from the Greek version of the Hebrew Scriptures, is a mistranslation, confusing the Hebrew word for "young woman" with the Greek word for "virgin". In context the verse from Isaiah (7:14) clearly intended nothing miraculous; a king's young wife would produce an heir to the throne who would rule justly. The misreading and misuse of the ancient text has caused skeptics problems for ages, but the myth of the virgin birth has been useful in some respects. In addition to reflecting the paradoxical attitude of Christians toward Jesus, the myth of the Virgin Mary has provided an opportunity to include ideal female qualities in the projection of human longing. In spite of all the attempts, ancient and modern, to think of God without the limitations of gender, God comes across in the tradition most of the time as aggressively masculine. The desire for tenderness, accessibility, nurturing, and mothering needs the feminine focus provided by the Virgin Mary.

Although the references to the birth of Jesus are troublesome, the statement that "he was crucified . . . suffered death and was buried" seems to cause no problems for skeptical people. They realize that the execution of Jesus of Nazareth was a historical event as well attested as anything else that happened two thousand years ago. They seem to have no difficulty in accepting the reality of Jesus' death and burial. What they sometimes miss, however, is that the significance of the death is not to be found in history but in religion. The Romans crucified thousands of criminals and revolutionaries, but their deaths have no impact on life today. The death of Jesus has impact because in that particular death we have a focus for our fear of dying and our need for courage in facing the inevitable end of living.

References to the death of Jesus may pose no problems, but the notion of Jesus rising from the dead presents an almost insurmountable barrier for many skeptics:

> On the third day he rose again
> in accordance with the Scriptures;
> he ascended into heaven
> and is seated at the right hand of the Father.
> He will come again in glory to judge the living and the
> dead,
> and his kingdom will have no end.

Many skeptics suppose that the first Christians claimed to have seen and touched the resuscitated corpse of Jesus of Nazareth. Such an assertion strikes them as a fraudulent claim invented to impress the gullible. They might not have such difficulty with the notion of Jesus rising from the dead if they looked carefully at the oldest written account of that event, the one quoted in the creed. It is found in St. Paul's first letter to the Christians at Corinth (15:3-8):

> For I delivered to you as of first importance what I also received, that Christ died for our sins in accordance with the scriptures, that he was buried, that he was raised on the third day in accordance with the scriptures, and that he appeared to Cephas, then to the twelve. Then he appeared to more than five hundred brethren at one time, most of whom are

still alive, though some have fallen asleep. Then he appeared to James, then to all the apostles. Last of all, as to one untimely born, he appeared also to me.

Several points are worth noting about this brief passage, starting with the use of the word "appeared". This is the language of dream and of vision. Paul does not use the language of objective experience; he does not say that anybody actually saw Jesus after Jesus had died.

Second, observe the sequence of people to whom Jesus appeared: (1) Cephas, also called Peter, (2) the rest of the inner circle of disciples, (3) the wider group of Jesus' original followers, (4) James, the brother of Jesus, who eventually took over the leadership of the church in Jerusalem, (5) the apostles, those sent out to tell the story, a different group from the original twelve disciples, and (6) Paul himself. Paul asserts that Jesus appeared to all of these people in the same manner. The experiences of Peter and the rest of the twelve soon after the death of Jesus were no different from that of Paul, which took place years later, or that of James, which occurred in between. Clearly, Paul did not think of the risen Christ inhabiting an ordinary human body before he disappeared into the sky. Instead, Paul is suggesting that in being "raised" Jesus was no longer limited by time, geography, and a physical body. Jesus could appear to anyone through a dream or vision or any other kind of experience that opened up a person's imagination to the presence of God.

Third, consider the repeated phrase "according to the scriptures". Paul's way of talking about his experience of Jesus is the result of his being immersed in the sacred writings of his people, the Jews. He used what had been written earlier to shape not only his descriptions of his experience but his way of thinking about what had happened to him. This is another clue that Paul knew he was expressing himself in the language of religion, not of objective history.

Paul did not invent the metaphor "raised" to describe Jesus appearing to his followers after his death. The disciples who witnessed the death of Jesus apparently were the first to employ the term resurrection, *anastasis* in the Greek of the New Testament. It means literally to stand up from a crouching or cowering position. If you put aside questions about what happened to Jesus, you can see that immediately after he died his disciples were crouching or cowering and that later they were able to stand up. Although the stories about what happened to his disciples following Jesus' death differ markedly in the three gospels that include such accounts, the three agree about the fear and discouragement suffered by those who grieved over the loss of their teacher. John pictures them cowering in fear behind locked doors (20:19). In Matthew's brief account, twice the followers of Jesus have to be told, "Do not be afraid 0 (28:5, 10). Luke tells about two of them trudging dejectedly back to their home village of Emmaus with no hope for the future (24:13-35). Then the next thing we know, these people who had been laid low by the death of Jesus were on their feet, changing the course of human history, and calling themselves "the body of Christ". It seems quite likely that we can find the origin of the resurrection imagery in the experience of the original followers of Jesus. They found themselves raised up to become the new body of Christ.

The myth of Jesus being raised from the dead provides a way, not only of talking about the experience of the original disciples, but also of looking at what frequently happens to people knocked down by events beyond their control or by their own inadequacies. St. Paul was raised up, and so was Sam, whom I mentioned earlier. Jesus being raised up reflects the eternal truth about human affairs, a truth that can sustain people when they feel defeated and a truth that can help them reflect on what has happened when they recover: people find themselves put back on their feet through a power that is not their own.

While many "resurrection" stories appear in the New Testament, only Luke includes the story of Jesus' ascension into heaven (Luke 24:51 and Acts 1:6-11, which was also written by Luke). Although in its most crude, objective form the ascension is offensive to most skeptics, the story points us in the direction of two valuable insights. The crudest presentation of his ascension is probably that of a mosque on the Mount of Olives outside of Jerusalem, where for a small fee the visitor can see the imprint the foot of Jesus made in a stone when he took off into the sky. If skeptics can put that kind of portrayal of the ascension out of their minds, they might find value in the two insights it suggests.

In the first place, the ascension suggests something important about the natural process of grief. When a member of our vestry killed herself, the community was so shocked and saddened that we invited her psychiatrist to meet with us after the Sunday morning memorial service we had held for her. At the conclusion of the meeting, the psychiatrist proposed that we gather again in a month or six weeks to talk further about our grief and about the person who had died. He said that in his experience people are often numb with shock for several days following the death of a person who had been important to them. Then there follows a period when the people are in grief and are constantly reminded of the dead person's absence. Finally, after a month or six weeks, people go through another kind of grief when they realize the dead person is really gone and they will have to let go of their mourning and get on with their lives. As soon as I heard those words, I said to myself, "Of course." According to Luke the ascension occurred forty days after Jesus died. The disciples were asked the same kind of question that every person in grief needs to hear after about forty days: "Men of Galilee, why do you stand looking into heaven?" The time had come to let go of their grief-stricken hold on Jesus and to get on with the business he had entrusted to them. The ascension is a reminder of what we have to do whenever someone dies.

Second, the ascension takes the resurrection one step further in setting Jesus free from first-century Palestine. The picture of Jesus going up from the place he had lived and taught creates a more vivid sense of Jesus being able to take the whole earth into his concern. Photographs from weather satellites have enhanced the power of this metaphor for us. From up there, the cameras can see everything that is happening on the face of the globe.

The idea of Jesus returning from "up there" to judge the living as well as the dead has captured the imagination of brilliant authors, like Dostoevsky, as well as of hare-brained preachers who scare people into believing the end of the world is at hand. Both are fascinated with the possibility of Jesus returning to judge the people who claim to live by the standards he established.

Most skeptics profess to have an aversion to judgment. To say someone is "judgmental" is to deliver the ultimate condemnation. Yet in every heart there is a longing to be tested and to be found worthy. If people did not have such a longing to be judged, why would so many be driven to prove themselves in athletic contests or business or politics or romance? People long for approbation as much as they fear condemnation, but they cannot set themselves up for the possibility of the first without incurring the risk of the latter.

A recitation of this portion of the creed may help skeptics to become honest about their desire for judgment. Once they admit they need judgment, however, they will have to ask the question, "Who will be the judge?" For Christians the answer obviously is that God alone can be trusted with such authority. They know that if they do not trust in the judgment of God, they will be subject to the manipulation of every authority around them. Everything from a neighbor's opinion to the supervisor's annual evaluation will have the power to give them or withhold from them a sense of self-worth.

St. Paul had a good grasp on the freedom that comes with acknowledging God's judgment:

> With me it is a very small thing that I should be judged by you or by any human court. I do not even judge myself. I am not aware of anything against myself, but I am not thereby acquitted. It is the Lord who judges me. (I Corinthians 4:3-5)

St. Paul is on to something important when he notes in passing that he is free not only from the tyranny of the judgment the Corinthians might lay upon him but also from the even more tyrannical possibility of judging himself. I will never forget a young clergyman shaking his head sadly and saying with genuine despair in his voice, "Everyone tells me I'm doing a good job, but I'm a failure by my own standards." St. Paul may have been supremely arrogant in many respects, but he never displayed the arrogance of that young clergyman; he never assumed that he had the authority to judge his own work or his own worth.

People who adopt St. Paul's attitude toward judgment can receive negative criticism without being devastated and positive criticism without being captivated. If they can locate the source of judgment beyond the human realm and beyond their own self-perceptions, they can evaluate what they hear about themselves and put to use what they find to be true.

After expressing our desire for judgment, the creed moves rapidly to a conclusion, gathering up other examples of our longing for a meaningful life and death:

> We believe in the Holy Spirit, the Lord, the giver of life,
> who proceeds from the Father and the Son.
> With the Father and the Son he is worshiped and
> glorified.
> He has spoken through the Prophets.
> We believe in one holy catholic and apostolic Church.
> We acknowledge one baptism for the forgiveness of sins.
> We look for the resurrection of the dead,
> and the life of the world to come. Amen.

"Spirit" is an almost universal metaphor for God: *ruach* in Hebrew, *pneuma* (from which we get pneumatic) in Greek, *spiritus* in Latin, and *gast* (or ghost) in Anglo-Saxon. The objective meaning of the word is the same in each language. All of the words originally meant air, breath, or wind. How air in its various forms became a symbol for the presence of God is not difficult to imagine. Air is invisible. Breath is essential for energy and for life itself. The wind carries awesome power.

Jesus also used the spirit metaphor as a reference to the gift of awareness. When he was trying to teach people and they were refusing to pay attention, not merely to him but to what was going on in their lives, he said, "Whoever speaks against the Holy Spirit will not be forgiven, either in this age or in the age to come" (Matthew 12:32). Or to put that observation about blasphemy against the Holy Spirit another way, if people refuse to be aware of what is going on within them and around them, even the Lord God in heaven cannot help.

The reference to the Holy Spirit in the Nicene Creed is also a reminder that the Hebrew Scriptures contain a wide variety of symbols for the experience of God—such as shepherd, king, lion, mother, and wisdom. Christians, however, settled on three others—Father, Son, and Holy Spirit— to highlight the special features of the story they wanted to tell.

By employing no fewer than three of the many possible metaphors for God, Christians follow the Hebrew tradition of recognizing that human beings experience God as complex and dynamic rather than as monolithic and static. Some medieval theologians wrote that the Trinity, as these three symbols came to be known in Christian shorthand, pointed to their understanding that "God is friendship." Nothing is wrong with the translation "God is love" for I John 4:8, but friendship catches more of the sense of interaction and community that are essential ingredients of the Christian life. The Trinity is the simplest way of projecting onto God what we have discovered to be true: life is bewilderingly complex and dynamic and takes on meaning only as we interact with other people within the context of a caring community.

By choosing those three particular symbols, however, the early Christians created problems for the present generation, especially for the skeptics who are also feminists. The three metaphors in the creed are decidedly masculine in the way they are presented. If the originators of the creed had known of our need for inclusive language, they could have added the obviously feminine "mother", or "wisdom", which is definitely feminine in Hebrew (see Proverbs 1:20,21). Or they could have used neutral words like parent and child and referred to the spirit as "it", which would be perfectly proper, since the word in the Greek of the New Testament is neuter.

Every generation in the church has different needs, and we have to make adjustments in the way we make use of our tradition. One way is to insist that we can with validity think of the Spirit in feminine terms. I like to think of the Spirit speaking with a woman's voice when prompting the prophets of old. I think the telephone company has a good reason for using a woman's voice in their computer-driven information service. Wisdom can best be internalized when presented in the tones that remind us of mother and our first teachers. For me the spirit of God is "she".

Another group of people who have problems with the Nicene Creed are those who have developed an anti-Catholic prejudice. They cannot understand why the prayer book refers not to the Episcopal Church but to "one holy catholic and apostolic church". Often they need to be convinced that this is not a reference to the Roman Catholic Church. Actually, the phrase is an indication that our belief, or confidence, does not rest in any human institution but in a vision of a church which never was nor ever will be on this earth. When we say "catholic", we are acknowledging a desire for a church that is universal and inclusive. When we say "apostolic", we are referring to our desire for access to dependable teaching that has been handed down through the ages by people committed to transmitting the truth.

Some people think of church primarily in terms of a building, while for others church means people. To think of church as a building is perfectly appropriate, since the word means literally "the Lord's house", but that meaning of church is obviously not what is intended here. Although it may be less obvious, church in this context does not mean people, either.

The church identified in the creed is neither building nor people, but a symbol of God's presence throughout the world in all ages. The building and the people provide an occasion for discovering the meaning of God's presence for ourselves. If we can discover that meaning in church, then we will have the security and the self-confidence to take life as it comes. We will not have to be defensive or hostile in the presence of strange or difficult people because we will not be easily threatened. Or as my teacher Charles Penniman put it, if in church we know ourselves to be God's people, we are free for "friendly mobility" throughout society.

Access to the security and self-confidence available through the church comes through baptism. In practical terms, acknowledging "one baptism" allows the Episcopal Church to accept into its ranks anyone who has been baptized in any Christian community. The Episcopal Church does not see itself as an exclusive organization in sole possession of the truth, but as one manifestation of the Christian tradition. It recognizes the validity of all the others, including their rites of baptism.

The final statement of the creed says, "We look for the resurrection of the dead, and the life of the world to come." When discussing resurrection and the possibility of eternal life, many skeptics have announced to me, "I don't believe in God, and I don't believe in life after death" as if the two were inseparable. I think the linkage is unfortunate. The two symbols are treated quite differently in the Nicene Creed. We believe in one God, but we look for the resurrection of the dead and the life of the world to come. Belief conveys the notion of trust along with a projection of longing, but looking suggests primarily the longing without the same kind of confidence.

The truth is that no one knows what happens to people when they die. One evening Stephanie Hallmark, a nine-year-old in my congregation, approached her father and announced that she had it figured out. "When you die, you go someplace else, or you come back again, or you just die dead." No more can be said with authority. All else is simply speculation. Obviously, people latch onto whichever of the three possibilities appeals most, and then they try to convince themselves that they know the truth and that the other two are wrong. In saying the creed, we admit that we know nothing for certain, but that the possibility of another life after this one has a certain appeal. The possibility gives us a way of holding in mind people who have already died and of imagining ourselves with them when our time comes.

Once skeptics discover that the Nicene Creed is an expression of human longing rather than a series of questionable propositions, they often discover that they can join in the recitation without feeling hypocritical or guilty. To get to the place where they can say the creed easily, however, may take some time. For a while, every time they get to the creed in the service they have to do a simultaneous translation of the religious symbols into language that makes sense to them, but if they stay with the creed long enough, eventually the ancient metaphors become part of their vocabularies and they can dispense with the translations. At that point the creed may become a useful expression of their own longing for meaning and for God.

Chapter 5 PRAYER—A Practical Possibility

Pat came to me because she was troubled by her relationship with her dying mother. Pat had resigned her position with a major museum to care for her mother, a cancer victim with only a few months to live. Pat had expected that the time they had remaining would be filled with tenderness and affection, but instead she found herself constantly bickering and quarreling with her mother. When I asked her what help she found in prayer, she quickly responded, "I don't pray anymore. Sometimes I wish I could, but I don't believe God exists. If there were a God, how could he possibly let such a wonderful woman die in the prime of her life, not yet fifty years old?" Like other skeptical people, Pat had occasionally thought wistfully about the possibility of praying, but she faced what seemed like an insurmountable barrier.

Obstacles to Prayer

Much as they might want to pray on certain occasions, skeptics find themselves faced with obstacles, some of which are formidable. They have to get past these barriers before they can learn to pray. Obstacles to prayer come in two varieties: the way people think about God and the way they think about themselves. Skeptics have identified both kinds of barriers when they have complained about the difficulty they have experienced in trying to pray.

God Doesn't Exist

The most obvious reason for not being able to pray is thinking that nobody is out there to receive the prayer and to respond. God does not exist. Even the thought that God may not exist deters some people from trying to pray.

When skeptics who are going through troubled times identify God's non-existence as their reason for not praying, however, I am immediately suspicious. Pat did not need much prompting from me to hear the anger in her voice. On reflection she discovered that her problem with prayer was not the question of God's existence but her anger with God for letting her mother die at such a young age. Assigning God to oblivion had been her unconscious method for getting even for all the pain God had caused her. Once she realized that her rage was an indication that she had an intense and intimate relationship with God, she could start to pray again.

For some skeptics, of course, the possibility of God's non-existence is indeed the barrier that must be faced. One skeptic, struggling to overcome her addiction, found that the second step in Alcoholics Anonymous presented a barrier to her progress: "We came to believe that a power greater than ourselves could restore us to sanity." When she complained that the program could be no help to her because she didn't believe in any such power, an older member counselled her, "If you don't believe, make believe." Countless numbers of skeptical alcoholics have found their way to sobriety by praying as if they believed.

"Make believe" may sound like difficult advice to follow if you have seriously considered the evidence and come to the conclusion that God does not exist. If you want to pray, however, you may profit from following the suggestion that Jesus made to "receive the kingdom of God like a child." Although you may not have used the skill in recent years, as a child you probably learned how to "make believe". Like riding a bicycle, making believe is something you never entirely forget how to do. When I was eight years old, my best friend and I once spent an entire afternoon in front of a toy microphone providing the news, performing soap operas, and giving out the commercials for an imaginary audience in radio land. When I was forty years old and wanted to pray in spite of my skepticism, I found that I could retrieve my capacity for make believe. Admittedly I was shaky at first and felt more than a little silly praying as if I thought someone were listening, but gradually I got the hang of speaking to an imaginary audience once more.

As I was learning to pray, I was encouraged by reading about the difficulties other people had faced in praying. I discovered that even people who had devoted their lives to prayer, and who are now considered saints, often went through periods in their lives when they felt like their prayers were addressed to empty space. What helped them was the same practice that sustains people in AA; they continued to pray as if they were confident that God was there for them.

God Doesn't Listen

Many people who have intellectually accepted the probability of God's existence still face a serious obstacle to prayer. They cannot pray because they think God is not listening to what they say. For them praying is like talking into a telephone that has gone dead. If they keep talking when they are not getting even a buzz or a click in response, they feel not only foolish but also frustrated. Often their feelings are directly related to their pictures of God at work.

A troubling thought to some people is that God could not possibly listen to all of the people in the universe talking at once. They picture either a jammed switchboard or a desk covered with telephones all ringing at once. This obstacle need not be too difficult to surmount, either, because the obstacle is of our own making. We become limited by the metaphors we employ to talk and think about what cannot be put into words. To think of God "listening" our minds naturally leap to human forms of communication, and we forget that when we speak of God "listening" we are using metaphorical language to express our longing for unity with the source of life. Listening is what people do and what animals do, but if God is God, what God does will always be a mystery to us. We have to use metaphors like "listening" to imagine the activity of God, but when we use the term as if it referred to an objective reality, we limit our access to God.

If you are troubled by the image of the jammed switchboard or the desk covered with ringing telephones, you must simply invent a new image of person-to-person conversation. The metaphor Jesus suggested was that of a loving parent. "Pray then like this," he taught, "Our Father, who art in heaven." Only he apparently did not use the formal, respectful title, "Father" but the familiar and intimate word in his language, "Abba", which should be translated with an English equivalent, like Papa or Daddy. To act as if they were having a confidential conversation with a totally wise and infinitely loving papa— one without the limitations of their natural fathers—works for some people, but not everyone. Some people do better with peer relationships. Those who are uncomfortable with the feeling of helpless dependency that sometimes arises in parent-child conversations may do better to picture themselves talking with an individual more like themselves, such as Jesus of Nazareth. Those who are more comfortable in an intimate conversation with a woman than with a man can envision themselves talking with Mary in any of the variety of roles in which she has been cast: virgin, sister, mother, widow, Queen of Heaven. If none of these images work, they can always have a conversation with one of the saints. I realize that skeptics brought up as Protestants may be horrified at the thought of praying to the Virgin Mary or to the saints, but if they are having trouble holding a conversation with God, they might try another image before giving up on prayer altogether.

Another approach to dealing with the obstacle of God not listening to you is to present God with your complaint about the way God seems to be treating you. That is the approach taken by the poet who composed Psalm 88: "Lord, why have you rejected me? why have you hidden your face from me?" As we all know, questions beginning with "why" are rarely requests for information but are usually indications of a complaint. I learned as a small child that if my mother said, "Why didn't you wash your hands before coming to the table?" she was not looking for an explanation but for a change in my behavior. The psalmist was using "why" in the same way we do, expressing disappointment and resentment. This approach has frequently worked for me. I find that sometimes the easiest way to start talking to God is to complain about God not listening. After talking for a time as if someone could hear my complaint, I realize that I might as well go on with the rest of my prayers as if someone were listening to them as well.

God Doesn't Answer

For some skeptics the observation that God does not seem to answer prayers troubles them even more than the experience of God not listening. They might feel frustrated and foolish talking to someone who is not "out there", but in spite of that difficulty, they think they could learn to pray if they could see some results. The author of Psalm 22 was complaining about the absence of a response:

My God, my God, why have you forsaken me?
and are so far from my cry
and the words of my distress?
O my God, I cry in the daytime, but you do not answer;
by night as well but I find no rest.

Most skeptics who have tried to reach out to God can identify with the complaint that God does not answer. The fact
that believers can point to occasions when God has answered
their prayers does not help skeptics to overcome this obstacle.
Sir Francis Bacon in 1620 penned the classical refutation to
the proofs offered that God answers prayers: "It was a good
answer that was made by one who when they showed him
hanging in a temple a picture of those who had paid their vows
as having escaped shipwreck, and would have him say whether
he did not now acknowledge the power of the gods,—'Aye,'
asked he again, 'but where are they painted that were
drowned, after their vows?'" Bacon was the godfather of
modern skepticism. He insisted that truth could be found only
through inductive reasoning, which is the process of making
careful observations, analyzing the data gathered, and then arriving at generalizations that are at best probabilities. Because
the minds of most skeptics seem to be programmed with
Bacon's type of logic, they cannot accept the anecdotal
evidence of believers trying to prove that God answers prayers.

Inductive reasoning about prayer leads the skeptic to a
disturbing dilemma. The skeptic must either pray as if God
were all powerful but answered prayers arbitrarily, if at all, or
as if God were limited in ability to respond but answered only
appropriate prayers, such as those for courage, perseverance,
and strength.

The trouble with the first approach is that you can easily
develop the attitude that God is capricious, cruel, and hateful.
A couple that I knew stood by helplessly while their only child,
a daughter in her late twenties, was slowly dying of a melanoma
that had spread throughout her body. When a well-meaning
friend told them that God might need such a fine young woman
with him in paradise, they were horrified. How could they
possibly find comfort by praying to a god who killed young
women for his pleasure? They tried hard to resist the notion

that the approaching death of their daughter was the will of God, but they could not shake the notion that if God is all-powerful, God either caused the disease that was killing their child or, if not that, refusing to intervene and allowing the disease to kill her. When other friends spoke to them about God's love, the anguished parents felt driven more deeply into despair. God certainly had shown no love for them or their daughter.

Because the notion of an omnipotent God frequently leaves people with the sense that God is cruel, many people have looked for solace in the second option, especially after reading Rabbi Kushner's book, *When Bad Things Happen to Good People*. Unfortunately, Kushner's approach to the dilemma also creates severe spiritual and emotional stress for some people who try to follow it. Take the mother whose sixteen year old son died in a boating accident. He had been out on the lake alone in a canoe just before dark. Nobody saw him tip over, and nobody could explain why he had not been able to swim the short distance to the shore, but he was dead. Having rejected the notion that tragedies are the will of God, she had absolved God of all responsibility, yet she could not help feeling outraged at the senseless death. The problem was what to do with her rage. She lashed out at her older son who should have been with the boy. She accused her estranged husband of neglecting the boy and so undermining his self-esteem that he didn't have any friends to take with him. She blamed the rescue squad and the emergency room staff for not reviving him. She had no place to focus her anger, and she also had no one to whom she could address her prayers. If God was not able to keep her son upright in a canoe on a peaceful lake, God did not have enough power to deserve her respect and worship.

In the midst of their anguish, the parents who thought of God as all-powerful and the mother who thought of God as limited made the same mistake, and it cost them what help they might have derived through prayer. They forgot that they could not define the reality of God by their opinions. They could not know for certain if God is all-powerful or limited, caring or capricious. Although childhood religious conditioning had shaped their attitudes, as adults they had chosen a way to hold God in their imaginations. Even when their idea of God was interfering with their relationship to God, they had decided to stay with a familiar attitude rather than to examine other ways of thinking about God.

These parents who were trying to cope with the loss of their children made exactly the same mistake that most people do under similar circumstances. In times of tragedy, most people find it all but impossible to examine and adjust their attitudes toward God. Skeptics interested in the possibility of prayer, therefore, would do well to ponder the dilemma in a period of relative calm and stability. I suggest that in their pondering they keep in mind the concept of paradox and the teaching of the Bible.

A paradox is literally two truths lying side by side. This concept is useful when dealing with our attitudes toward God, which we form in our ignorance as we face the ultimate mystery of life. While we observe that some people have found it useful to think of God as all-powerful, we also note that others have found the exact opposite to be true: they have taken comfort in the concept of a limited God. The skeptic, therefore, can embrace the contradiction in the knowledge that pushing either position without the corrective force of the other can result in a devastating separation from God. Had they been able to embrace the paradox, the parents of the dying daughter could have held God accountable for the life of their child, praying as if God could save her, and at the same time could have concentrated their realistic expectations on finding the strength to get through the ordeal. The mother whose son drowned might also have been helped by a grasp of the paradox. If she had been willing to blame God for the accident, she might not have hurt the people around her with her misplaced anger, and she might have developed a respect for God once her anger had spent itself. At the same time she might have prayed as if God could not have been expected to intervene, but still could always be counted on to comfort and support her.

The Bible presents a variety of ways for dealing with the dilemma of God's power versus God's goodness, but the idea of a limited God is quite foreign to the biblical tradition. God is never pictured as being limited by nature or by circumstances. Most of the older parts of the Hebrew Scriptures follow the line that if the people of Israel, especially their kings, do what God commands, God will answer their prayers. If they do what is evil in God's sight, God will refuse to answer their prayers and will find ways to punish them. God upholds the righteous and destroys the wicked. The book of Job, however, challenged that theory. That magnificent poem, a reflection on an old folk tale about the suffering of an innocent man, identifies the dilemma and the shallowness of the usual explanations for suffering. The poet does not solve the dilemma posed but instead embraces the paradox. The poem ends with an assertion of Job's innocence and an affirmation of both the power and the love of God.

Much as I appreciate the serious theological struggle in the poetry of Job, for me the usefulness of the Bible in helping with prayer is not to be found in religious philosophy but in the stories of people in conversation with God, including Job. All of the great characters in the biblical stories bring their complaints to God, but the one whose words I find most moving is the prophet Jeremiah. Here is one example, taken from the twelfth chapter, of how Jeremiah addressed God:

> You are righteous, O Lord,
> when I complain to you;
> Yet I would plead my case before you.
> Why does the way of the wicked prosper?
> Why do all the treacherous thrive?

This prayer well illustrates the capacity for paradox the ancients demonstrated. In their experience God ignored obvious injustice and oppression, but they prayed as if God were ultimately responsible for everything that happens. By being totally forthright in their complaints, the characters in the Bible stories could carry on an intimate relationship with God while enduring tragic events. This biblical way of approaching the obstacle to prayer created by God not answering is available to modern skeptics who are willing to accept the paradox.

I Don't Deserve a Hearing

Just as images of God create obstacles to prayer, so do self-images. Some skeptics cannot pray because of the ways they

picture themselves. Much as they might like to pray, they do
not because they think they do not deserve to be heard.

One time I offered to pray with a fine old gentlemen who
was in the hospital suffering with heart disease. He refused
my offer saying, "I never prayed before so it wouldn't be right
to start now." Then he added, "I'm not as good a man as you
may think I am." At first hearing, this explanation of the
obstacle to prayer sounds quite humble. Here is a man near-
ing the end of his life who had never bothered with prayer so
he believes it would be presumptuous to start praying when he
has finally reached a problem he cannot solve. At the same
time, he admits that he has had moral failures that render him
unfit for conversation with God. These sentiments may sound
humble, but if you listen carefully you will detect signs of arrogance. The man could not pray because he had not earned
the right to approach God. He did not want God to accept
his prayers as a favor, for that would put him in God's debt,
and he did not want to be beholden to anyone.

Some people may be genuinely humble. They may have
made a realistic assessment of their faults and know that they
have no basis for making a claim on God's love or care. If so,
they are in good company. A central element in Christian
worship from the beginning has been the confession that "we
are not worthy to gather up the crumbs under thy table", let
alone to claim that we deserve to be fed. In the Christian tradition nobody deserves a hearing; everyone approaches God as
an unworthy petitioner.

I Don't Know How to Pray

Many skeptics do not pray because they never learned how.
They may even have looked for someone to teach them from
among the ranks of people who should know how to pray only
to discover that many professional Christians do not know how
to pray, either, but are reluctant to admit their ignorance. That
was the position in which I still found myself twenty years after
beginning my theological studies. In my search for guidance
I came across Geoffrey Curtis, an elderly monk of the Community of the Resurrection in London. Impressed by his piety
and wisdom, I ventured to ask him why he supposed that for
generations clergy had not been taught to pray. His answer

was that people who know how to pray become spiritually independent. They do not need the authority of the theological school, or the monastery, or the bishop in order to feel secure with God. It is not in the self-interest of anyone in the church hierarchy to assist the clergy in becoming spiritually independent, and it is not in the self-interest of the clergy to foster a similar independence among the laity.

The Benefits of Prayer

The obstacles to prayer are real. God may not exist, and even if God does exist, God may not listen to prayers. If God does listen, God still may either not answer any prayers at all or just not answer the prayers of people who do not deserve an answer. The methods suggested for getting across the barriers may just be tricks to play on oneself, mental gymnastics which at best are a harmless pastime and at worst are a way of avoiding personal responsibility. The benefits of prayer must be real to justify the investment of time and energy in an endeavor beset by such ambiguity. For me the benefits of prayer are real, and skeptics can verify these benefits through their observations and experience.

Encourages Perspective

People create the most trouble for themselves when they adopt a narrow point of view. They sometimes fail to recognize what they really want, they fail to understand other people, and they fail to live up to their responsibility. By praying about their concerns, however, even skeptics can gain the perspective they need to live happy and productive lives. They can discover what really matters to them; they can increase their sensitivity to other people; and they can identify specific areas where they need to exercise responsibility.

When a young man discovered that his wife was pregnant for the first time, he offered a prayer of thanks and then prayed that God would grant him a son. Having said quite honestly what he wanted, he realized that the sex of the child was not as important to him as having a healthy child, so he amended his prayer to remove the sex qualification. On reflection, he realized that he was praying not so much out of concern for the unborn child as from anxiety about the risk his wife was taking in giving birth to a baby, so he revised his prayer again to begin with a plea for her safety. As he sat quietly, he found a still deeper level of desire: what he really wanted was the capacity to join his wife in the joyful adventure of childbirth and to find the courage necessary to be with her in any pain or sorrow the future might hold. By telling God what he wanted, the expectant father discovered what he really wanted.

A stockbroker had an appointment with a difficult but important client. She was sure that the investor wanted to see her because the stocks in his portfolio were not keeping up with the rising market. This particular client had a way of insinuating that the poor performance of any stock was the broker's fault. Discovering that the more she thought about the approaching meeting the more angry and anxious she felt, the broker decided to include the difficult client in her prayers. She began by trying to hold the client in mind without asking for anything in particular, just trying to form a desire for the client's well-being. As she began to calm down, a few thoughts about the client emerged then and a few other thoughts came up on the drive to the office. To begin with, the broker was not sure what the client actually wanted. The broker had just made a guess, and the guess may have been based more on the broker's feeling of guilt for not being attentive to this client's investments than on anything the client had said. Then the broker recalled the hints the client had dropped about trouble that had nothing to do with investments: a marriage that had fallen apart and a daughter suffering from depression. She also began to wonder if the client's rebarbative manner might not be a cover for tender feelings and insecurity. When the time for the appointment came, the broker was no longer expecting an enemy but another human being, with anxieties and longings similar to her own.

When you pray for other people, you have to make an real effort if you decide to repress thoughts about what responsibility you might have for the person in your prayers. When I pray for my widowed mother, I cannot help but do a mental check to see how recently I have called her and how long it has been since we have been together. The same principle can be seen at work in a congregation that prays regularly for the poor people of their city. Ways to help with food or jobs or clothes arise in the minds of the worshipers; they often cannot help having such thoughts as a result of the prayers. They may ignore their thoughts and never take any action, but that is another problem. The prayers bring their responsibility to mind by bringing to them a new perspective on suffering in their city.

Reduces Stress

Prayer can reduce physical and emotional stress in three ways. First, it provides an outlet for frustration and rage. In James Clavell's novels, members of an old Scottish clan sometimes return to their homeland from adventures in distant parts of the world because they need time with the "screeching tree". They would curse and shout and rage at the tree until they were exhausted, and then calm again, would face their trouble with renewed energy. Everyone needs a system something like this to let off stored-up negative energy. Complaining to God about misfortune and blaming God for trouble that cannot be traced to another human being provides a vent for the emotional steam that can reach dangerous levels during periods of frustration.

Second, prayer provides a way of managing anxiety. Anxiety falls into two categories: worry over things you can take care of yourself, which can be a positive motivating force, and worry over things beyond your control, which can be debilitating. When you pray as if God is going to answer your prayers, you can separate your anxieties into two piles, one for you and one for God. An unemployed systems analyst, for example, set aside time to pray as part of his preparation for an interview with a consulting firm that did the kind of work that most interested him. He wanted the person who was going to interview him to start the day off well with a good breakfast, a pleasant goodbye from a loving spouse, and a relaxed trip to the office. He wanted the interviewer to be open and receptive and to recognize the gifts he could bring to the company. As he prayed about what he wanted, the systems analyst recognized that the emotional and mental state of the interviewer was absolutely beyond his control. He put his anxiety about the interviewer into God's pile. He still had enough anxiety left to make a sizable pile for himself, but through prayer he knew that appropriate anxiety could be transformed into useful energy. The anxiety in his pile could help motivate him to do his homework on the company, to re-write his résumé to fit the company's objectives, to dress well for his appointment, and to speak articulately during the interview. By praying about what he wanted, he was able to keep the motivating anxiety for himself and to put the debilitating anxiety into God's hands. As a result of praying, the systems analyst went to the interview with his anxiety working for him and without the look of desperation in his eyes that has caused so many people to miss out on an employment opportunity.

Third, prayer provides a discipline for mental and physical relaxation. Certain techniques of contemplative prayer, or meditation, have an immediate calming effect on the whole body, including the brain. By clearing their minds of obsessions and anxious thoughts and by slowing down their breathing, people who pray can actually lower their blood pressure. Over a two year period, my dentist participated in a campaign to reduce hypertension by taking the blood pressure of all his patients on their semi-annual visits so he could warn them if they were in danger. This happened to be the same two year period in which I was learning to pray. After my fourth blood pressure check, the dentist gave me a puzzled look, and asked, "Do you know that over the past two years your blood pressure has fallen from the high end of normal to the low end of the scale?" I laughed and admitted that I had been cheating; I had been doing contemplative prayer exercises while he took my blood pressure to see if what I had heard about the calming effect of prayer was verifiably true. It is.

Strengthens Bonds of Affection.

Praying has a way of binding people together. When my father was slowly dying from brain cancer, I was surprised at first by how warmly pleased I felt when members of the congregation told me that they had remembered him in their prayers. Although I would have rejoiced in a miraculous cure, my pleasure did not arise out of an expectation that their prayers would save my father's life but out of the knowledge that they cared enough about me to spend a moment or two holding in mind a man they never met because they knew of my grief.

I also find that when the situation is reversed, I feel close to the people for whom I have prayed. Each day I pray for the people I know who are suffering or sick or troubled, and in those moments I sometimes feel almost as I do when I visit them at home or the hospital: my concern and affection is intensified by the contact.

Of course, people do not have to be in difficulty to be appropriate subjects for prayer. My three daughters are grown up and living in distant cities. Although they left home many years ago, I still miss being with them. Praying for them makes them seem less far away. In prayer, time and geography lose their power to separate us from the people we love.

Just as personal prayer can strengthen the bonds of affection between individuals, corporate prayer can enhance the love that binds together the members of a worshiping community. In the middle of the Sunday morning worship service, the liturgist offers people the opportunity to pray aloud or to ask for the prayers of the congregation. Joan offers thanks for the birth of grandson. Frank asks for our prayers as he and his family set off for two months in Africa. Jack asks help for the hatred he feels in his heart for the two young men who mugged him Saturday evening. Jeanette wants the congregation to pray for her sister and brother-in-law whose marriage is in trouble. As the community joins each of these people in their prayers, many hearts go out to them. People sense the concern around them and feel less alone with their burdens and their joy.

Enhances Enjoyment

Prayer can make an already pleasant life even more enjoyable. Through prayer I can take delight in each event at least three times: anticipating the occasion, experiencing the moment, and giving thanks for what has taken place. Several times a year my wife and I get together with the same group of friends for a meal and an evening of conversation.

In anticipation of the evening, I enjoy praying for each of the people who will be present and asking God's blessing on our gathering. I nearly always enjoy the get-togethers themselves, and then I savor the memory as I give thanks the next day for the privilege of spending time with such good people.

I realize that you can find other ways to take three-fold pleasure in each planned event in your life, but I know of no better way. Pleasure is enhanced by talking about what is about to happen and about what has taken place. Little children are usually more straightforward about asserting their need to tell about what is going on in their lives. I remember my second daughter in tears because her two sisters managed to tell me all about their trip to the zoo leaving her nothing to tell. In seeing her tears, I realized that my need to tell is as great as hers. But to whom can an adult tell about all the joys of life? Spouses, friends, bar tenders, colleagues—all have a limited capacity for hearing about other people's happiness. They are often better at listening to tales of trouble because another person's distress confirms them in their sense of superiority or comforts them in their own sorrow.

When my first book was published, I became painfully aware of how few people want to hear about another person's joy. On the day of a parish dinner dance I had received advance copies of the book. I moved around the party joyfully brandishing a copy of my new book, foolishly expecting an enthusiastic response from the people to whom I spoke of my long- awaited success in getting published. No one was exactly frosty, but neither was anyone as eager to listen as I was to tell. God turned out to be the only one to whom I could speak about my great delight without feeling that I was imposing.

Frees Creativity

Prayer can set free creative resources in the mind that otherwise would not be easily accessible. Much has been written in the past few years about how to gain access to both sides of the brain and how to call up insights through imaginative preparation for sleep. Most of these books and articles purport to be scientific, but the methods they suggest sound suspiciously like prayer.

By praying you can break out of circular thinking that has your mind going in a downward spiral or linear thinking that has taken you straight up against a brick wall. A man who sold newspaper advertising was miserable in his work, bored and depressed. He always dreamed of buying his own paper in a small town, but he could never accumulate sufficient capital. What he really wanted to do was spend the rest of his life fishing, but he could not afford to retire. He felt trapped. The more he thought about his situation, the worse he felt.

Prayer has a way of setting the mind free from such traps. By telling God about his distress and about what he really wanted out of his life, the salesman could set aside the sense of misery that was blocking his thinking. He became aware that staying put and buying a paper were not his only options. He then looked for ways to use his interest in fishing to make his present job more interesting. He came up with the idea for his paper to promote a fly-casting competition, which would promote interest in the recreational resources of the local area, stimulate readership during a dull time of year, and boost advertising from sporting goods shops as well as from the motels and restaurants that would benefit from the influx of visitors. Both the advertising manager and the publisher liked the idea, and with the support of the managing editor and sports editor the plan was successfully launched.

Nourishes Faith

When I suggest that prayer nourishes faith, I am using "faith" in the biblical sense: the capacity to affirm reality, including the reality of one's longing for God.

Regular prayer can often help put a stop to self-deception. In all of the examples used so far to illustrate the benefits of prayer, self-deception was causing trouble. Self-deception is an avoidance of reality. To the extent that a person stops avoiding reality, that person is adopting a faithful approach to life.

One reality many skeptics try hard to avoid is their longing to live in harmony with the infinite, but once they accept the reality, skeptics need a way to express the longing. Prayer can provide a way for the honest expression of the hunger for contact with the ultimate mystery that lies behind the universe. One of my most cherished prayers begins, "O God, our great companion, lead us ever more deeply into the mystery of your life and ours." That petition has helped to keep me honest in the times when I feel least sure about God's existence and am inclined to deny my longing for God. What I really want is to be led more deeply into the mystery. By continuing to pray, my faith is strengthened in the sense that I become less inclined to repress my "rapturous amazement at the harmony of natural law", as Einstein called it, and less likely to deny my desire to be at peace with whatever superior intelligence may be the source of the harmony.

Guidelines for Skeptics

In drawing attention to some of the benefits of praying, I have hinted at several requirements for a satisfactory experience with prayer. For the convenience of skeptics who want to try praying, I have extracted six rules for prayer from my reading and my experience:

1. Be disciplined. Learning to pray requires as much discipline as learning to play the piano or learning to practice medicine. For me, the three elements of the discipline are time, place, and posture. Of course, people can pray any time and any place and in any physical position, but few people learn to pray unless they start with a set routine.

Decide on where you want to fit prayer into the rhythm of your life. Determine a schedule: once a week, once a day, several times a day. Choose times when you feel most certain that you will not be interrupted. In Islamic countries, everyone stops to pray five times a day, but that is not the case in the western world so you have to plan more carefully to find regular times that will not disrupt the people around you. Most people find that first thing in the morning or last thing before bedtime works best because prayer can fit into already established patterns of washing and tooth brushing. Others find that lunch hours or coffee breaks at work provide the best fixed times for prayer.

Finding an appropriate place is also necessary for establishing a routine. Jesus said, "When you pray, go into your room and shut the door and pray to your Father who is in secret." Not bad advice. To approach the one who is hidden, people need to hide themselves from other eyes and ears. Prayer works best in privacy. The Celtic monks and nuns went to great lengths to find remote places where they would not be distracted in their prayers, but most people today must be content with a room and a door to shut out the rest of the world. The room can be a bed room, living room, office, or even a "closet", as the older English versions translated Jesus' words. Some people find that having a special focus in the room helps them to pray: an icon, a cross, a candle—something to remind them of the task at hand.

Because the mind is part of the body, physical posture has a significant influence on the experience of prayer. If you are serious about praying, you may need to experiment a little to find a posture in which your body can be relaxed and your mind alert. What is most important is to find a posture in which you can breathe correctly, that is use your abdominal muscles to control your diaphragm so that you can regulate your breathing. That must have been important to the ancients, who identified the diaphragm, or *phron* as they called it, as the center of decision-making and who used "breath" as a primary metaphor suggesting the presence of God. In correct breathing, the abdominal muscles are used primarily in exhalation. By tightening those muscles and pushing them back toward the spine, you force the diaphragm up and expel the air; by allowing them to relax, you let the diaphragm drop and create a vacuum in your lungs that draws in a new breath. You can do that standing, sitting up straight in a chair with a firm seat, sitting cross-legged on a cushion or on the floor, lying flat on your back, kneeling upright, or kneeling with your forehead on the floor. The important thing is to find a posture that works for you. If you are having trouble regulating your breathing, you can get coaching from any good voice teacher or yoga teacher.

2. Be persistent. According to John's gospel, Jesus said, "If you ask anything in my name, I will do it." Absurd as those words may sound in the ears of a skeptic, similar teachings attributed to Jesus appear throughout the New Testament, such as: "Ask and it will be given to you; seek and you will find; knock, and it will be opened to you." The experience of most skeptics suggests that either such assertions are false or that the disciples were supposed to ask for only those things they knew they would get anyway. After reading though everything

Jesus was supposed to have said about prayer, I came to a different conclusion: Jesus taught his followers to pray as if God
would grant everything they asked because he wanted them to
pray persistently no matter what happened. My conclusion
rests to some extent on the parable that appears in the
eighteenth chapter of the Gospel according to St. Luke.

> He spoke to them in a parable to show them that they should
> keep on praying and never lose heart: 'There was once a
> judge who cared nothing for God or man, and in the same
> town there was a widow who constantly came before him
> demanding justice against her opponent. For a long time
> he refused; but in the end he said to himself, "True, I care
> nothing for God or man; but this widow is so great a nuisance
> that I will see her righted before she wears me out with her
> persistence."'

You must remember that a parable is not an analogy. You
are not necessarily like a wronged widow and God is not necessarily like an unjust judge, but the story illustrates the point
Jesus was trying to make: the necessity of persistence in
prayer. Nearly everyone who tries to pray becomes discouraged at times and wants to give it up, but the benefits of
praying can only be gathered by continuing with the discipline
through the periods when the whole business of praying seems
to be useless and ridiculous. I have a notion that the absurdity
of praying—in the light of our knowledge that prayer is not
likely to change anything—helps open our minds to the ultimate absurdity of our existence and to the mystery that is the
source of the universe.

3. Be Honest. Many skeptics were brought up with such
good manners that they assume God expects them to be polite
when they address God with their concerns. Being polite
means withholding all negative comments—any hints of
blame, disappointment, or anger. Being polite means refrain-
ing from making any requests that might be construed as selfish or uncharitable. Being polite also means being less than
honest. When you are less than honest with God, however,
you may unconsciously develop a contemptuous attitude. You
act as if you could fool God with a facade of good manners
and as if God would be upset with you for telling the truth. I
think prayer works best when you act in just the opposite way,

when you act as if God knows everything and cannot be fooled, and when you act as if God is sufficiently generous and secure to accept whatever you have to say without being offended.

In trying to adopt the attitude that God cannot be fooled and knows everything, some people have wondered why they should bother putting their thoughts into words. The reason is that you do not pray for God's sake but for your own. You can find analogies on the human level for the impact on the speaker of putting thoughts into words. My wife knows I love her, and I know I love her, but when I tell her that I love her I become more open to the experience of our mutual love. My wife knows that I hate being late for a party, and she knows when I have become angry because she has taken so long to dress that we will be late, but unless I identify my anger with at least a few words, my anger will separate us and spoil the evening.

In all healthy relationships, people speak the truth even when the truth is well known. The opposite is also true. In families where relationships are destructive, people refuse to speak the truth that is known to all. In one family, everyone knew that Mother made more money than Dad and that she made all of the important decisions, but everyone pretended in polite conversation that the father was the boss. Such an atmosphere breeds misery as effectively as stagnant water breeds mosquitoes, but no one in the family would admit how bad things were until the son, the older of the two children, ran away from home just as he was about to begin his senior year in high school. When we use the human analogy of truth telling to illuminate a possible relationship with God, it seems fairly obvious that in prayer honesty is the best policy.

Prayer works best when you picture God in the way that most appeals to you and say whatever is on your mind. You tell God exactly what you want, what worries or angers you, what pleases or delights you, what makes you sad or sorry.

4. Be positive. Disciplined, persistent, and honest prayer can be dangerous for the practitioner who does not follow the rest of the guidelines, especially this one. Unless you maintain a positive frame of mind while you are praying, you can

become obsessed with what is troubling you. A first-year law student, like most of her classmates, was extremely anxious as examination time drew near. Hoping to do her best, she was willing to try anything, including prayer. To her dismay she discovered that the more she prayed, the more anxious she became. When she tried to pray harder and longer, she became even more upset. The problem was that she had concentrated all of her energy on the area that troubled her most, to the point that the anxiety took over her whole life. For prayer to sustain you in trouble, you have to say what you want, imagine the best possible outcome, and then move on, looking for what you can do to improve the situation and leaving the rest to God.

Unless prayer is positive, it holds another danger: some kinds of trouble are seductive. Prayer can be an excuse for savoring both the trouble and the guilt that may accompany it. A married psychotherapist who considered himself to be a deeply spiritual person became sexually attracted to one of his female colleagues at the clinic. Instead of discussing this complication with his supervisor, he decided to handle his feelings in prayer. He carefully examined all of his impressions of the young woman. He reviewed all of his fantasies of caressing her and making love to her. As a result of his prayer life, he became alienated from his wife and practically fell into his colleague's arms when they found themselves alone late one evening after the clinic had closed. Had his prayer been positive, he would have identified the troublesome area, admitted his inappropriate passion, decided what he needed to do about it, and quickly turned to other subjects.

If you are not conscious of the need to be positive in your prayers, you can easily become obsessed with any kind of trouble: sickness, marital discord, financial failure, or the death of a parent, just to name a few. In addition to being positive, you can also help yourself from falling into the trap of obsessive concerns by sticking to the next two rules as well: be submissive and be receptive.

5. Be submissive. Surrendering their will to the will of God has been the path to serenity for believers since ancient times.

That path is also open to skeptics, even if they are not certain that God is responsible for anything that happens in this world.

I can offer my own experience as an example of what I mean about submitting yourself to the will of God. The biggest disappointment in my life was not being elected dean of a theological school. The search process had taken over a year, as the field was gradually narrowed to just two candidates, a seminary professor and me. After having been ardently pursued, I had persuaded myself that I was the right person for the position. I was crushed when I learned that the board of directors had elected the professor instead of me. Once the decision was made, however, there was nothing I could do to change it. The only aspect of the situation over which I had any control was the attitude I would adopt to deal with my bitter disappointment. As I saw it, I had four options: (1) I could decide that my failure was all my fault and blame myself, or (2) I could decide that I had been badly treated and blame the students, faculty, and board members who sided against me, or (3) I could decide that my defeat was the result of fate or random bad luck, or (4) I could accept the decision as God's will. Actually a good friend offered a fifth option by suggesting that the vote was engineered by the Devil, but since I do not like dualism—looking at the world as if it were a battle ground between two divine beings—I did not give real consideration to the possibility of a diabolical plot.

As I thought about my options, the first three held no promise of peace. Blame and fatalism lead to bitterness and depression, while accepting what happens as the will of God can lead to healing and new possibilities. In accepting the decision as God's will, I discovered several reasons why the job might not have been good for me or the school: I hate fundraising, academic types frequently bore me, and I need a community with more continuity than a student body to sustain me. I also found new reservoirs of energy and enthusiasm for parish ministry, the work I had been doing, once I accepted my place as God's will. I do not mean to suggest that I convinced myself that I know for certain what is on God's mind. I would never make such a claim. I do know, however, that my life works best when I act as if what cannot be changed is God's will and then submit myself to what God has ordained.

In deciding to accept what happened as the will of God, I was probably influenced by the well-known prayer composed by the Christian theologian, Reinhold Niebuhr:

God, give us grace to accept with serenity the things
that cannot be changed,
courage to change the
things that should be changed,
and the wisdom to
distinguish the one from the other.

Like anything else of value, Niebuhr's prayer can be misused. The desire for serenity can lead you into the danger of passivity. You can easily distort the purpose of the prayer by externalizing what you mean by "things" and by using the prayer as a way of avoiding responsibility. That is, you can act as if all situations can be divided into just two mutually exclusive categories: those things which you cannot change and those things over which you exercise control. The truth is that most situations fall somewhere in between. In most areas of your life you may not be in control but you can exert influence. You cannot change other people but you can change the way you treat them. You cannot end corruption in city hall but you can refuse to bribe the building inspector.

You may find it tempting to seek serenity by passively ignoring the things that come within your sphere of influence, but that approach is rarely successful, as the husband of an alcoholic wife discovered. Before the two of them began their vacation one summer, he was clear that he could not control her drinking. They went off to a cabin with a private beach on a secluded lake and relaxed happily for a few days with her drinking seemingly under control. Then another couple arrived unannounced, wanting to spend the night. They were friends of his wife, drinking chums in her college days. By five in the afternoon the three of them were already well under the influence. They did not manage to get anything on the table for supper until after ten. As soon as the dishes were washed, the husband excused himself and went to bed. About two o'clock in the morning, he woke up with the realization that he wife was not beside him. About an hour later she staggered into the bedroom and collapsed fully clothed onto the bed.

In recounting the event to his counselor, the offended husband was convinced of his own innocence and righteousness: he could not control his wife's drinking and the conduct her drinking produced. By adopting that attitude, however, he had failed to note how much satisfaction he got out of feeling superior to his wife and to recognize any of the points in the unhappy event when he could have exerted influence. He could have objected to inviting the guests to stay; he could have insisted on eating early; he could have stayed at his wife's side, knowing she was out of control. None of these actions would have assured a happy outcome, but they would have kept him from being an accessory to his wife's delinquency.

The prayer for serenity helps only when you realize that "the things that should be changed" are frequently the things that are within. Working on these things can lead you to a more responsible exercise of your influence over the things you cannot change by yourself.

6. Be Receptive. Finally, in order to get the most out of prayer, you must learn to be receptive. Useful conversation requires listening as well as speaking. I do not mean to suggest that if you listen, you will hear a voice answering your prayer. In fact, if you do hear voices, I suggest you contact your nearest mental health center immediately. But I do mean that in prayer you need to take time to be quiet and to listen. Listen for challenges to your ideas; listen for new possibilities; listen for reassurance and for comfort.

Learning to be receptive in prayer can take some time and concentration. Receptivity requires a particular kind of praying, in the Christian tradition usually called contemplative prayer and in the Eastern religions usually referred to as meditation. Contemplative prayer was of particular interest to Celtic Christians in the fifth and sixth centuries and is an important, but frequently neglected, aspect of our Anglican heritage. We have reason to believe that the Celtic Christians received their approach to contemplative prayer from the deserts of Egypt and Syria to which Christians had fled in their desire to be alone with God. We know something of the ways in which the desert monks practiced contemplative prayer, and some of those ways are open to you without the necessity of abandoning your present life.

The point of contemplative prayer is learning how to be calm and quiet. What I said about the discipline of prayer— time, place, and posture—is even more important for contemplative prayer than for prayer that is more like a conversation, sometimes called "intentional prayer" to distinguish it from the contemplative variety. In contemplative prayer, correct breathing is essential, but it takes practice. The practice itself, however, can have a calming effect on both the mind and the body. You can just sit quietly and concentrate all of your attention on your breathing, making sure that you breathe slowly and deeply. When other thoughts come into your mind, you can note them briefly and then turn your attention back to your breathing.

The trouble most people have with trying to be quiet is that just thinking about breathing leaves too much mental capacity free to do other things. When I stop to listen to my own mind, I can usually hear at least five channels playing at once, all competing for my attention. One is the worry channel, suggesting that the cough I have had for the past two weeks is probably a symptom of lung cancer. The second is the nagging channel, reminding me that I have not paid my American Express bill and have not written to my children. The third is the garbage channel; it sometimes plays reruns of the movie I saw last week, which is not so bad, but it often puts on continuous tapes of singing commercials that I heard in my childhood, like "Pepsi Cola hits the spot/ Twelve whole ounces that's a lot." The fourth channel reveals the immediate present.

The reason some people like playing bridge or working on computer problems is that they can turn up channel four and drown out the other three. While their attention is fully occupied by the business at hand, they do not feel anxious or upset about anything substantial. Contemplative prayer works in a slightly different manner. In contemplative prayer, you give channel three something else to play.

The desert fathers spoke of using breathing to place a prayer in your heart that would always be there for you to listen to when you were quiet even for a moment. That is what I mean by re-programming channel three. The early Christian monks recommended that people put into their hearts a simple petition called the Jesus Prayer. You can come find it in various forms. A very short version appears in the prayer book: "Lord, have mercy upon us." The longest form I have come across is: "Lord Jesus Christ, Son of God, have mercy on me, a sinner." If you use the long form as part of your prayer discipline, you can say the first half to yourself as you inhale and the second half as you exhale. Some people find they can concentrate best, however, by saying the prayer aloud, in which case they inhale slowly and then say the whole prayer as they exhale. Either way, the idea is to concentrate on the prayer to the exclusion of other thoughts by repeating the prayer over and over.

Once the Jesus Prayer becomes a part of you, it is always available. I use the prayer in rhythm with my breathing when I am swimming, or walking, or doing stretching exercises. The prayer can keep me from wasting energy on worry or silly fantasies, but it leaves me free to be sensitive to what I called channel four, my immediate surroundings.

I confess that when I first started saying the Jesus Prayer many years ago, I felt silly even though I was all alone. At that point in my life I had not tried to pray for about fifteen years. As a theological student I had tried to pray occasionally, because I thought clergymen were supposed to, but I had given it up as a lost cause. For reasons I cannot explain, in spite of feeling foolish, I persisted in repeating the Jesus Prayer over and over each morning. After about two weeks of this, one morning I was startled to discover that I had stopped saying the Jesus Prayer and that I was talking to God as if God were an old and trusted friend. Because of that experience, I cannot separate the two kinds of prayer in my daily routine. Contemplative prayer makes it possible for me to say what is on my mind, and intentional prayer lets me get everything off my chest so that I can be quietly receptive.

I am convinced that even the most skeptical people can learn the art of both intentional and contemplative prayer if they think the benefits of praying might make the effort to overcome the obstacles worthwhile. I realize that some skeptics might scoff at my suggestions. They can accuse me of simply putting a religious gloss on a program for stress management. I am also aware that some believers may accuse me of reducing the radical demands of faith by suggesting that people can find value in prayer without believing. My position, however, is that the approach to prayer I have outlined requires faith in the sense that is embodied in "amen", the root of the Hebrew word that is translated "faith". Amen means "yes". Faith is an affirmation of what is. To pray with the attitude I have suggested is to accept both reality and our capacity to cope with reality as if everything has been given to us by God.

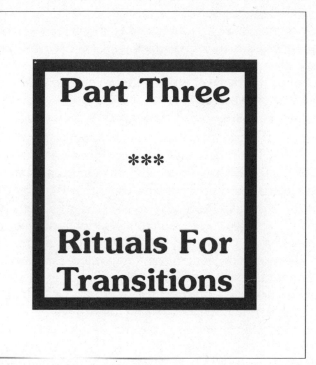

Part Three

***

Rituals For Transitions

The unconscious need for ritual often dominates the behavior of even the most skeptical people. Few of them will let a birthday pass unnoticed or will agree to a marriage that begins simply with the signing of legal documents. What is true in private life is still more obvious in public life. Every important transition is marked by a ritual: the inauguration of the president or of a governor, the opening of a post office or a highway, the awarding of diplomas or academic degrees. The unconscious desire for ritual may also be a major factor in the widespread addiction to televised sports, which provide catharsis through ritual forms of combat.

More often than not, the people who are observing or engaging in these modern rituals have no idea that the rituals have evolved from forms once in the exclusive province of religion. Marriages and the anniversaries of births were observed by giving thanks to God. People entering public office dedicated themselves to the service of God. Building projects when completed were dedicated to the glory of God. People who received academic degrees were accepting not only their credentials to teach but also God's blessing on their work. The drama of the battles between the archangel Michael and the devil, and between St. George and the dragon, provided Christians with experiences of ritual combat.

Recognizing neither their instinctive desire for ritual nor the origins of the rituals they employ, people often create two problems for themselves. First, they plan rituals that are inadequate to handle the emotional freight of the transitions that concern them, and second, they fail to derive the benefit of inherited rituals because they do not understand their meaning. For example, in planning a fiftieth birthday surprise party for her husband, one woman wanted to make the evening a totally happy occasion with a series of tributes as well as presents from his friends. Afterwards she could not understand why the event left her husband feeling depressed and quarrelsome. If she had paid attention to the meaning of one ritual act that she had included—asking her husband to blow out the fifty lighted candles on the cake—she might have known what was bothering him. In ancient times, candles were a symbol of life. By blowing out the candles, the guest of honor at a birthday celebration was acknowledging the inevitability of death. Most people turning fifty have unsettling thoughts about their own mortality. When those thoughts are denied or suppressed by an inadequate or misunderstood ritual, the result is likely to be irritability and depression. Rituals work only when they catch up the full range of emotions produced by the transition.

People who are interested in learning how to plan and to use rituals that work would do well to study the best available source of rituals: the Book of Common Prayer. This book of ritual resources demonstrates the genius of the Episcopal Church and the wisdom of the Anglican tradition. The prayer book provides for transitions from one day to the next, one week to the next, and one season to the next; for beginning marriage and for taking on the responsibility for rearing a child;

for facing surgery or death; for getting through illness or bereavement.

Many skeptics have been attracted to the dignified atmosphere that can be created for the marking of a transition by the lofty cadences of the Book of Common Prayer, but the real genius and wisdom of the Episcopal prayer book lie not so much in the language but in the substance of the rituals. In every service, the prayer book allows people to give voice to their sorrow as well as their joy, to acknowledge tragedy as well as triumph, to express their fear as well as their courage, and to admit their shame as well as their confidence.

The meaning of the rituals provided by the prayer book, however, may be no more obvious to the participants than is the blowing out of candles to most of the guests at a birthday party. Although the language is English, the words are often used to convey ancient Hebrew or Greek verbal images found in the Bible. It takes a little work to set aside the customary way of using particular English words and to uncover the ancient symbols they are intended to convey. It also takes a little effort to discover the origins of particular ritual actions so that they can be thoughtfully employed in contemporary circumstances. I have tried to make some of that work a little easier for the skeptical reader.

Chapter 6
THE CELEBRATION AND BLESSING OF A MARRIAGE

Even people who pride themselves on their disdain for organized religion often show up at church when they decide to get married. When asked what a church wedding would mean to her, one young woman apologetically replied that she "just wouldn't feel married if they went to a justice of the peace." Her fiance added that he was willing to go along with the church idea, since he had always supposed that if he ever got married he would get married in church.

These two young people, thoroughgoing skeptics on most matters of religion, gravitated by instinct to the church when they decided to get married. According to Milton Cotler, a sociologist I met in the late sixties, their instinct was a healthy one. In that period of cultural upheaval, when many people were trying to deny the value of all tradition, Cotler attended a wedding that a couple intended to celebrate without using any ritual whatsoever. They rented a hotel banquet room, laid out food and drink, and waited to see what would happen when their family and friends arrived. What happened, according to Cotler, was that most of the guests began drinking compulsively and soon fell into shouting, quarreling, and weeping. The wedding was like a small-scale riot. "Of course," he said, "such a disaster was predictable. You can't have a wedding without ritual. All of the emotions brought to the surface at a wedding must be channeled or they will overwhelm the gathering. Ritual provides the channels."

The emotional atmosphere at a wedding is always highly charged. As a new commitment begins, old relationships are breaking up or being redefined. That is as true for the couple in their thirties who have been living together for five years as it is for the recent college graduates who kept separate addresses before their marriage. Skeptical couples as well as believers come to church to get married because they sense that this is an appropriate place to help them manage a major transition in their lives.

The Prior Marriage Paradox

One of the ideals of the Christian tradition is that marriage is a permanent arrangement. The church has maintained this tradition even though we know that many people who present themselves to be married have been previously married and divorced. For a long time divorced people who wanted to get married in the Episcopal Church had only two options: they had to go through a quasi-legal proceeding to prove that the prior marriage was not a real marriage, or they had to get married somewhere else and later ask to have their marriage recognized by the church. Neither of these options was very attractive since they both required a certain amount of duplicity on the part of the couple. How can a person honestly say that a marriage which lasted eight years and produced three children did not really exist? How can people honestly get married in a community church knowing that they are simply trying to get around the rules of the church they prefer? Our present arrangement is that the bishop of any diocese at the request of any of the clergy can grant permission for divorced people to be married in the church. Having given up the duplicity, we now live with the paradox: we absolutely hold marriage to be a life-long union between husband and wife, and we absolutely hold that all sin, failure, and negligence must be forgiven.

When church leaders become obsessed with either side of the paradox they can cause grave difficulty. Churches that cling too tightly to the absolute indissolubility of marriage become dangerously oppressive. They encourage women to stay in marriages with men who beat and abuse them. They withhold the gifts of the church from divorced people and so make them feel more guilty than embezzlers, swindlers, or even murderers, all of whom can be married in the church without regard to their past. The church can add to people's pain when their marriages are breaking up by rejecting their pleas for understanding.

By being understanding about divorce, however, the church may inadvertently encourage people to separate when they are simply moving through one of the painful transitions in married life. All marriages fall apart periodically, at fairly predictable times. Some get put back together because the husband and wife believe that they have made a life-long commitment to each other.

Changing Attitudes toward Marriage

A reading through the marriage service in the 1979 Book of Common Prayer may produce a few surprises. At all points the man and the woman use identical language in making their vows. At one place the woman speaks first and at another place the man speaks before the woman. Obviously the prayer book reformers have made a real effort to treat men and women as equals, a value widely endorsed in late twentieth-century society. While rejecting the popular notion of marriage as a temporary arrangement, the prayer book service reflects other shifts in values held by society.

Just how accurately the marriage service reflects changes in cultural norms becomes clear by a brief look at earlier versions of the ritual in the Anglican tradition. For example, one purpose of marriage, according to the 1549 Prayer Book, was "for a remedy against sin, and to avoid fornication". The first American prayer book, published in 1789, avoided all mention of the purposes of marriage. In colonial America as well as in the continuing life on the frontier through the nineteenth century, people saw marriage not so much as a way of keeping their sex drives from running rampant but as a means of economic survival. Life on the edge of the wilderness required partnership and a division of labor, but apparently the church leaders did not want to make such an assertion in the ritual. Our contemporary understanding of marriage as being primarily companionship, however, was incorporated into the ritual in the most recent revision.

The appropriate relationship between a husband and a wife has also changed over the ages. Sixteenth-century brides in England who were married using the 1523 Salisbury Rite promised "to be bonny and buxom in bed and at board". In those days, "buxom" had not acquired its connotation of being full-breasted but meant pliable. The proper attitude of a woman to her husband was at all times to be cheerful and submissive. That language was not picked up by the 1549 Prayer Book, but part of the thought was contained in the bride's vow "to obey and serve" her husband. We should note that obey did not originally mean "to do as you are told" but meant rather "to listen attentively". Still, before that promise disappeared from the prayer book in 1928, the intent clearly was that the husband was boss.

Although the wife promised to obey and serve her husband, she received a promise from him that put their partnership in balance. According to the 1549 Prayer Book, when he gave her the ring, the husband pledged: "With this ring I thee wed; this gold and silver I give thee; with my body I thee worship; and with all my worldly goods I thee endow." Just think. The man exists exclusively for his wife's sexual pleasure, and everything he owns as well as everything he acquires is destined for her benefit. In the early versions of the prayer book a difference existed between the sexes, but a certain rough parity was established.

Over the centuries that parity gradually eroded as the man's ring vow was shortened. First to go was the direct reference to gold and silver. The Americans then dropped the phrase about using his body to worship his wife. Next came the clamor to eliminate all mention of "worldly goods". Gradually during the late eighteenth and the nineteenth centuries society was developing a certain squeamishness in speaking about financial and sexual matters openly in church. An even more profound shift was taking place in the attitude of men toward women. As women began to agitate for equal political rights, the men who controlled the legislatures here and in Britain retaliated by stripping women of their financial and property rights. No one knows how long that trend might have continued, had not President Woodrow Wilson sided with the women's suffrage movement in order to win female support for his war in Europe. As a result, women not only won the right to vote, but were also able in 1928 to eliminate the woman's promise to obey and serve her husband from the Episcopal prayer book. The latest American version of the marriage service now has unisex vows, accurately reflecting our present social climate.

A quick look at the marriage service reveals that a couple makes not one, but two sets of vows. The reason for this apparent redundancy lies in the origin of the present service. Originally the church had two separate rituals, one for betrothal and one for the marriage itself.

The purpose of the betrothal service was to make certain that the proposed marriage met with the approval of all concerned. The ritual was held in view of the public so that all could see if the man and the woman clearly gave their consent to the marriage. Contrary to the popular view of our day, parents in earlier times could not force their daughters into marriages. The women as well as the men had to give their consent to the marriage in a public place where their fathers would not be able to apply any obvious coercion. Another reason the ritual was public was to test the eligibility of the two people for marriage. Did the man have a wife in another village? Were the two people too closely related? Were both of them mentally competent?

As communications improved and as the right of individuals to choose their own marriage partners became absolute, the need for a separate betrothal service disappeared. People are naturally conservative in liturgical matters;   however, rather than abandon the betrothal service, they added it to the marriage rite.

They probably had another reason for wanting to retain the public declarations of consent to the marriage. In giving their consent, the man and the woman made promises to their relatives and friends about how they would treat each other once they were married. Marriage is not just a covenant between the two principal parties, but is also a contract between the couple and their community. The couple agrees to a standard of behavior, and the community agrees to support them in this way of life.

The service begins with the betrothal ritual. In its present form this ritual is a re-enactment of the couple's engagement. This is ritual drama presenting to the public an already established situation that is the necessary condition for marriage.

The Exhortation

The first words in the liturgy are those of the celebrant, reminding the gathered congregation about the nature of marriage. In this opening statement, the celebrant declares that "marriage was established by God in creation." That phrase reminds me of a discovery I made a few years ago when I was reading the works of a noted ethologist. Having studied human mating habits as a zoologist might observe other animals, he had come to the remarkable conclusion that human beings appear to be genetically programmed for pair bonding. Scientists and church people have found different ways for saying the same thing: marriage appears to be part of the natural order of things.

In describing marriage, the celebrant refers to "a wedding in Cana of Galilee." This is a reference to a Bible story that appears only in the Gospel according to St. John. It appears in the second chapter, before Jesus has begun his public ministry. Jesus, along with his mother and some of his friends, is attending a wedding feast when disaster overtakes the celebration: they run out of wine. At the urging of his mother, Jesus saves the day. He tells a servant to fill with water six large stone jars, which would hold altogether about 120 gallons, to dip out a little, and to take it to the master of ceremonies. When the master of ceremonies tastes the water, he discovers that it is now wine, but not ordinary wine. He proclaims to the bridegroom, "Every man serves the good wine first; and when men have drunk freely, then the poor wine; but you have kept the good wine until now."

Putting aside all arguments about the historical accuracy of the account, we can ask ourselves what the Christian community who cherished this story found of value in it. One theory is that John's gospel was written and edited in the Christian community at Ephesus and reflects the concerns of this particular group of people living in the midst of pagans whose primary deity was Dionysus, the god of the vineyard and the wine vat. Christians may have told the story to remind themselves of the Jewish origins of their wedding customs and to assert that Jesus was now the Lord of all life, including their festivities. For them marriage was not simply one person moving in with another, but a major transition, one that called for great celebration. They wanted to be careful, however, to assert that their festivals were not part of the bacchanalian tradition, but were an acknowledgment that the Lord Christ approved of their rejoicing on such momentous occasions.

The celebrant makes another biblical reference in declaring that marriage "signifies to us the mystery of the union between Christ and his Church." This expression we might call a reverse metaphor. Early Christians developed a sense of intimacy with God through what they knew of Jesus. In searching for a vivid analogy from human experience to express that sense of intimacy with God, they naturally thought of marriage. They were well aware of the observation made in the second chapter of Genesis that when a man and a woman are married they become "one flesh"; that is, every thought, attitude, or feeling on the part of one may have a profound effect upon the other. Through their life in the Christian community these early followers of Jesus found a similar closeness with God (see Ephesians 5:21-33).

The metaphor that early Christians used to express their theology, however, suggests as much about their attitudes toward marriage as it does about their understanding of God. They apparently saw in the desire of a man and a woman to know each other intimately—to explore each other's bodies and minds—a reflection of their longing to know the mystery of the universe. They knew that while marriage could not save them from anxiety and despair, marriage could reveal to them their search for what might sustain them in times of adversity. They saw that the quest for mutual fulfillment in marriage reflected a desire to be connected with God.

The celebrant is using another biblical image in calling marriage a "holy union". In the Hebrew scriptures the word "holy" usually refers to a particular kind of experience, one in which people find themselves beckoned to a new venture but terrified of the possible consequences. In that moment they find themselves trembling in awe before the mystery of their own existence. When a man and a woman come before the altar to make their vows of marriage, they may find their knees shaking, their hands trembling, and the palms of their hands becoming damp with perspiration. These physical reactions to the moment are appropriate signs that the two people are encountering the Holy. They are beckoned to a new and better life as partners, but if they are not aware of the possible disastrous consequences of such a union, they simply do not know what they are doing.

The Charge

The celebrant then turns from the congregation to the couple and reminds them about the nature of the decision they made when they became engaged. The most important task undertaken by a couple contemplating marriage is determining if the marriage can be accomplished "lawfully". This word encompasses a great deal more than the word "legally". Lawfully in this sentence stands in parallel with the phrase "in accordance with God's Word". Both refer back to what the Hebrew Scriptures call the Torah. Translators nearly always use the English word "law" to stand for *torah*, but the translation is sadly inadequate. When the Jews call the first five books of the Bible the Torah, they know well that besides some legal precepts, the Word of God contains poems, legends, history, and myths. Like almost all Hebrew words, *torah* is based on a simple root. The root in this case is a verb meaning "the hunter hit what he was shooting at." From this same root evolved the Hebrew words that we translate as "parents", which occurs only in the plural, and "teacher". Parents, teachers, and laws have one thing in common with the image of a hunter's arrow finding the target: their purpose is to help people find their fulfillment, to help them become the individuals they were intended to be.

A lawful marriage, therefore, is one that allows both partners to become the people they really are without being warped by the desires and demands of the other. When people become engaged, they had best be aware that what they see is what they will get. Any intention of making the other over into a more fit spouse will lead to misery.

The Declaration of Consent

N., will you have this man to be your husband; to live together in the covenant of marriage? Will you love him, comfort him, honor and keep him, in sickness and in health;

and forsaking all others, be faithful to him as long as you
both shall live?

By responding in the affirmative to this question, the woman
makes a promise to the community about the way she intends
to treat her husband when they are married. Then the man
makes the same promise using similar language.

When church people use the word "covenant", they mean
something more than a contract or an agreement. In the
Hebrew Scriptures, God was often pictured as a benevolent
monarch who established the terms of his relationship with his
subjects through a covenant. When we speak of marriage as
a covenant, we are reminded that marriage is more than a legal
contract and that something more than grit and determination are required in making this agreement work. That "something" has been variously called grace, gift of God, or the help
of a higher power.

The biblical term behind the word "comfort" also means
something other than what is most often implied when we use
the word in English. In the context of the marriage ritual, to
comfort does not mean to make another person feel better, to
soothe or console. The Greek word, in fact, provides a lovely image of what a marriage is to be. The word is pronounced
"para-kaleho". *Para* means "alongside", as in paralegal or
paramedic, referring to people who work alongside lawyers or
doctors. *Kaleo* is a verb meaning "to call". Literally, the question is, "When he calls, will you come to his side?" In some
English versions of the New Testament, the word is translated
counsel instead of comfort, but neither attempt produces the
image originally intended. Married people cannot always
make each other feel better. Frequently they cannot even understand each other. But each can come alongside the other
when called.

A study of ancient business documents has revealed the
original meaning of the New Testament word we read as
"honor". The word frequently appeared in jewelry transac-
tions and apparently meant to place a high value on something. To honor another is to treat that person as being of
great value. The promise in this case is that no matter how
disappointed or angry one partner becomes with the other,
that person will do or say nothing that in any way makes the

other look cheap or of little consequence. If you have ever been around married people who demean each other, you will appreciate the significance of the promise to honor each other being made to the whole community.

The best interests of the community will also be served if those being married fulfill their promise to "keep" one another. In this promise "keep" is not being used in the sense of possess but of care for, protect, preserve from all harm.

Although the people gathered for a wedding can easily see how their interests are being protected by most of the clauses in the betrothal vows, they sometimes have difficulty with the final promise—"forsaking all others". Notice that this promise has no escape clause. No exceptions are permitted. To marry is to forsake all others. Obviously marriage is a sexually exclusive relationship, but marriage is exclusive in other ways as well. Marriage is the primary relationship; all others can hope for no better than second place. The claims of parents, employers, clients, colleagues, friends, and even the children of this or prior unions must never be put ahead of the legitimate requirements of the marriage partner.

This is one place where the Christian view of marriage is at odds with the culture, particularly when marriage and career are in conflict. For many people, the purpose of marriage is to advance careers. When it ceases to do so, the marriage has to go. Others look on marriage as a refuge from the battles of the work place; in which case any turmoil in the marriage itself is cause for resentment and reason for termination.

This promise assumes that the gathered community of friends and relatives believe that it is in their best interest for the couple to put their marriage ahead of all other obligations. If the wedding guests do not understand that they are involved in a counter-culture ritual, the celebrant has to tell them that, in the long run, they will all benefit from supporting the claims of the marriage partners on each other before their own demands.

After both the woman and the man make their promises to the congregation, the celebrant asks those assembled to make a promise to the couple:

Will all of you witnessing these promises do all in your power to support these two persons in their marriage?

This new version of the marriage rite makes explicit what in previous versions of the prayer book was only implicit. The purpose of inviting people to the wedding is not only to enhance the celebration but also to gain support needed for the new undertaking. The promise suggests an important principle: married people need the help of other people to make their marriage work. Since not everyone sees marriage as a permanent arrangement, couples who intend to stay married need to choose their friends carefully in order to develop a supportive structure that can see them through difficult times. They need married friends who will demonstrate by their behavior the value of keeping their marriage vows, as well as people who will tell them the truth and refuse to listen to one of them complain about the other.

I have seen the difference telling the truth can make in a marriage. A host at a party noticed that a married couple, long-term friends of his, were engaged in a bitter exchange of demeaning comments delivered from behind tight smiles. The host turned to them and said, "I don't like the way you two are treating each other in my house." That is all he said. He did not try to straighten them out. It was enough. On the way home the couple had a long talk, confessing to each other how unhappy they had both become with their constant bickering and sarcastic exchanges. Within a week they had engaged the services of a marriage counselor, and within a few months their marriage was back on track. Unfortunately, some people who have good intentions about being supportive to their married friends have been misled by the notion that they can always be helpful by being a good listener. Often listening to a married person's complaints about the marriage can be very destructive. By listening you not only re-enforce the complainer's sense of being in the right, you also drain away some of the energy that should be going into a solution to the problem. Good friends will not listen to a woman complain about her husband or a man about his wife, but instead will suggest that if the complainer cannot deal directly with the problem, the complainer should get some professional coaching from a minister or therapist.

The Presentation or Giving in Marriage

The custom of the bride being given in marriage dates back to Anglo-Saxon times, when all individuals were required to live in families. The family was responsible both for the protection of its individual members and for their behavior. For example, if a person stole a neighbor's horse and disappeared with it, the family of the thief would have to make restitution to the family that lost the horse. In a time before the development of police forces and ready access to courts of law, the system of family structure gave early English society its only hope for a reasonably ordered existence. To make the system work, any family that took in a stranger and kept him for three days became responsible for him as if he were a family member. No one was permitted to live outside a family, so when two people married, one of them had to change families. Usually, but not always, the bride joined the family of her husband. The ritual signifying that change was the bride's father escorting her to the altar and leaving her there with her new husband. By this act the father renounced all claims on his daughter's loyalty and all responsibility for her protection and her behavior.

In modern times this ritual act has taken on a significance that is more emotional than legal. Often marriage makes a radical, but appropriate change in relationships between adult children and their parents. This can be a painful, as well as a joyful, experience for a father who understands that he is letting his daughter go to another man. Walking with her to the altar and announcing that he is giving her up can help him manage the feelings he has about this transition.

Of course mothers as well as fathers may experience this sense of loss, and the parents of the groom may have feelings much like those of the parents of the bride. In fact, in ancient Israel the separation of a man from his parents received all the attention in the lore surrounding marriage: "Therefore a man leaves his father and mother and cleaves to his wife." Because many people present at the wedding may be going through a painful transition, the new prayer book makes provision for members of both families to present the man and the woman to be married.

The Marriage

The man and the woman then face each other. First the man takes the woman's right hand in his and makes his vow to her. Then the woman makes the same promise to him, using similar language.

> In the name of God, I, N., take you, N., to be my wife, to have and to hold from this day forward, for better for worse, for richer for poorer, in sickness and in health, to love and to cherish, until we are parted by death. This is my solemn vow.

When I read over the marriage service prior to my own wedding, one part of the vow made no sense to me: "for better for worse, for richer for poorer." I thought people made vows to cover contingencies. I understood why I had to promise that I would stay married to this woman even though our circumstances became worse and we had less money to live on. I grew up during the Depression, and I know what stress unemployment and poverty can put on a marriage. What I did not understand was why I had to promise this woman that I would stay with her even if things got better and we eventually had more money.

Charlie Smith, the clergyman who prepared us for marriage, enlightened me. Before becoming a professor of New Testament, he had been the rector of a church in Wellesley, Massachusetts, a wealthy suburb of Boston. He told us that in his experience more marriages broke up when things got better and people got richer than the reverse. In the years that have followed, my observations have borne him out. Couples who struggle though the strain and deprivation of graduate school break up just as they get established in their professions. People who slave away for years restoring a town house in the inner city separate just when the house is finished. A husband and wife have everything they have dreamed of— children launched, the house paid for, a place in the country, successful careers—and they decide on a divorce. So the burden of this vow seems to be: "I will stay married to you even though things get better and we get richer."

If the husband and wife keep their vows, and if neither meets with a fatal accident, the marriage in all probability will end when one dies following a terminal illness. Most couples face illness and death the way they have learned to deal with life and health, but they still make choices that will determine the quality of the dying person's last days and the quality of life for the survivor. When I was at a formative period in my marriage and in my ministry, I was profoundly influenced by the way two couples in my congregation dealt with terminal illness. One couple showed me what I hope to avoid at all costs, and the other provided a pattern I will do my best to duplicate.

In the first case, the wife called to ask that I visit her husband in the hospital. She said that he was dying of cancer, but that I should not mention this fact to him because he would not be able to handle the information. I went to see him several times. Once when we were alone in the room, he confided in me, "I know I am dying, but please don't tell my wife. She couldn't take it." Not knowing any better at the time, I became a participant in a charade that lasted until his death. We all pretended that he was getting well and would be home soon. He died utterly alone, living a lie that separated him from his wife and denied him the comfort she might have offered. As a widow, the poor woman was inconsolable. Having decided to cope with death by fraud, she had lost her husband six months before he died and had not provided herself with a way to grieve.

In the second case, it was the wife who was in the hospital. I learned that her breast cancer had metastasized and that she was not expected to live. When I stopped by the hospital to see her, I found her husband seated at the bedside. I had a strong sense that something was happening that did not include me, so I made a hasty retreat, but as I was leaving he asked me to meet him for a beer later in the evening. When we met, he confirmed my sense that I had blundered into an experience that was both profound and intensely personal. They had been talking about her death. She had told him how much she hated to leave him all the responsibility for their teenage daughters and their younger son. He had told her how much the future without her frightened him. They had held each other and wept. Then they had begun making plans for the immediate future. When he finished describing their conversation, he looked at me and said, "You know, whether she lives or dies, I wouldn't trade that experience for anything. We have never been so close."

To keep the vows until parted by death may well mean that a married couple will be upholding one another through the dying process. They cannot choose to live forever, but they can decide how they will cope with death when it appears imminent for one of them.

The nature of the bond required to sustain a couple through sickness until death is stated in two ways in order to avoid misunderstanding: "to love and to cherish". The word "love" has always caused problems in English because we use it to stand for two quite separate ideas. Most often love means an overwhelming feeling of affection and desire for another person. When the word appears in the New Testament, however, it means a conscious choice to act in a caring manner without regard to the feelings one might have for the other person. The prayer book adds the word "cherish" here in parallel with the word love so that everyone present will know that the second meaning is intended.

The problem about the double meaning of love has been around for a long time. The translators of the King James Version of the Bible were so concerned about the possibility of misunderstanding that when they came to the thirteenth chapter of St. Paul's First Letter to the Corinthians they refused to use the word love and substituted "charity". Modern versions of the New Testament use love, but the very popularity of the passage at weddings suggests that people are reading into it inappropriately romantic connotations.

Romantic love is not entirely within our control. It is as John Updike wrote, "a matter of pheromones, an obscure fit of neural notches." That kind of love produces a measurable substance in the blood stream, one of the neuropeptides that controls emotion. No one can honestly promise to be in a particular emotional state in regard to another person for as long as they both live. Nor can a person honestly promise another never to fall in love with someone else. Clearly the marriage vow speaks of something more important than feelings over which we have limited control. The vow is about behavior.

To promise the cherishing kind of love is to pledge constant concern and kindness without regard for transitory feelings. To promise the cherishing kind of love is to vow that falling in love with other people will not result in genital sexual relations with them. People who cherish their marriage partners may not always be able to control their feelings, but they do not let their feelings control their sexual behavior.

If two people keep the promise to cherish each other even at the times when they are no longer romantically in love, something wonderful often happens. They fall in love with each other again and again. When two people treat each other lovingly in spite of their feelings, they are likely to be surprised by moments of romance and affectionate desire, especially after surviving the first ten years of marriage.

The Giving of Rings

Marriage, among other realities, is a financial and sexual partnership. The vows that went with the exchange of rings in the earliest English versions of the marriage service made that more explicit than the present language, but the intent is the same. As I noted earlier, the first prayer book specifically mentioned gold and silver. Those words are a reminder that the ritual then included an actual exchange of money. Earlier still, people getting married brought to the church all of the worldly goods with which they would begin married life. For people of modest means, that meant bringing in such things as a plow or a wheel barrow, pots and pans, or even clothing. People who were financially better off brought their wealth in more easily transportable form: gems, jewelry, and coins. All of their worldly goods were blessed as part of the marriage service.

Now we generally follow the custom of offering just a small representation of each financial estate, a ring, to be blessed. The point is the same, however: marriage is a financial partnership. As a rule people get more upset about money than about any other area of married life. Money appears to be a form of spiritual energy that can have powerful positive or negative influence on people. How the husband and wife manage their money will to a large extent determine the life they make for themselves.

The Prayers

The promises the couple has made to the congregation and to each other are sensible and realistic. They provide an approach to marriage that can make the partnership infinitely rewarding to both of them. Yet the vows are also very difficult for most people to keep. At this point the best support that the people gathered together can provide is to pray for the newly married couple. Skeptical people often object to prayers, but I have never had even the most skeptical bride and groom object to being prayed for at their wedding. This may be an occasion parallel to the often made observation that there are no atheists in foxholes.

All of the prayers are quite appropriate for the occasion, but one strikes me as deserving of special attention since the thoughts it expresses are not found elsewhere in the service:

> Give them grace, when they hurt each other, to recognize and acknowledge their fault, and to seek each other's forgiveness and yours.

"Grace" refers to that gift of strength and courage greater than that which we can conjure up for ourselves, but which we frequently require. Notice that the word is not "if", but "when". Married people with best of intentions and good will are bound to hurt each other from time to time. On such occasions, the only way out of the misery created is for them to "acknowledge their fault". For some of us, being right can easily become more important than being in relationship with the person to whom we are married. Finding fault in someone else can also be more attractive than looking at what responsibility we have for whatever is troubling at the moment.

The literal meaning of the New Testament word translated as "forgiveness" is "release". To forgive a debt is to release a debtor from the obligation to pay. In a marriage, people can easily use their hurt as leverage to punish the offending party. There is some satisfaction in that position, but it keeps the two people separated and miserable. Seeking forgiveness only makes sense in a situation where each person knows the other will always be willing to let go of the lever and release the offending one from a position of weakness.

Sometimes, however, the forgiveness of your spouse is not enough to put you back into harmony. Maybe you think that you have been so awful that you deserve to be punished, deserve to be miserable. That position has a certain appealing arrogance, but the long-term effects can be devastating to the individual and to the marriage. Or maybe you just feel stuck with a burden of guilt so great that your spouse cannot lift it from your shoulders. In order to get out from under excessive guilt, skeptical people must learn to act as if God can release them from the burden of their past wrongs.

While everyone else remains standing, the husband and wife kneel for the final two prayers. The practice of kneeling dates back to ancient times when subjects knelt before their sovereign to demonstrate both their loyalty and their trust. Kneeling demonstrates loyalty by putting the subject on a lower plane than the monarch and trust by offering the back of the neck to the sword in the confidence that the blade will not fall. When the newly married couple kneel, they are demonstrating their loyalty to the one in whose name they made their promises and their trust in the help that one may give them to keep the promises they made.

After reading through the marriage service, skeptical people may realize that Christian marriage is not so much a matter of believing as of behaving. Skeptical people, who want to stay married and who know they will need help in keeping a promise to do so, can in good conscience have their marriage celebrated and blessed in church.

Couples who want to get married in an Episcopal church but do not belong to one should start looking well in advance of their wedding date. Some Episcopal clergy will not officiate unless at least one of the people getting married is a member of the church, and those clergy who are willing to preside at the marriages of non-members usually require no less than a month for pre-marital consultations. The engaged couples who get the most positive and helpful response from clergy are those who start attending the church and who make a financial commitment to it long before they bring up the subject of a wedding. Episcopal clergy often feel misused by people who want only an attractive setting for a wedding and who care nothing about the meaning of the ritual or the wisdom of the Christian tradition. People who demonstrate that they are serious about receiving support for their marriage through participation in the rituals of the church are much more likely to receive a warm response.

Chapter 7
THE BIRTH OF A CHILD—Holy Baptism

The second time in their adult lives that skeptical people often request the services of the church occurs when a child is born. They call the church to ask about getting the child "christened" or "baptized". If they use the latter term they are likely to get a more friendly response than if they use the former. Most active Episcopalians think that christening is for naming ships and baptism for people. Actually, "christen" comes from the Anglo-Saxon *christnian*, meaning "to make a Christian", so it is too bad that Episcopalians have abandoned the term to sailors, but that seems to be what has happened.

Even if skeptical people get past the barrier of terminology, they may be further put off by the less than enthusiastic response of the church to their interest in baptism. They may even find themselves being quizzed as to the reason for their interest. Before calling the church, skeptical people would do well to think through their reasons for wanting to have their child baptized, not only for the purpose of impressing the church with a thoughtful answer but also for the sake of their own integrity. The most obvious reasons for being interested in baptism may not be the real reasons.

One of the most frequent reasons given for wanting to have a child baptized is: "The baby's grandparents are going to be in town next weekend, and we thought it would be nice to get it done while they are here." Another goes like this: "The baby is almost two months old, and if we don't get it done pretty soon, we won't be able to get her into the christening gown that both my mother and I wore." To many active church people, especially clergy, these seem to be pitifully superficial and woefully inadequate reasons for requesting what the prayer book calls "full initiation by water and the Holy Spirit into Christ's Body, the Church", but if both the church people and the skeptics took time to look behind the words, they might discover fears and longings of a substantial nature.

Fears

The reason for wanting to perform a ritual centered on the baby when grandparents are in town may well reflect some sense of inadequacy felt by the new mother and father. After all they have read about the baby's personality being formed in the first years, or even months, of life, they wonder if they will be able to create the environment necessary for the child to develop in a healthy way. If both the mother and father will be working full time and leaving the child with someone else for most of the day, they also may wonder about how the parental substitutes are going to treat their child. Behind this wondering may be a genuine fear that the baby will not receive enough love, or the right kind of love, and will develop serious psychological and developmental problems.

Even if the parents have some confidence in their nurturing abilities and in their capacity to find adequate day care, they may fear the hazards of life over which they have little control. I remember not long after our first child was born going in to have one last look at her before taking myself off to bed. As I stood gazing intently at this beautiful little creature in her crib, I started to cry. At first I had no idea why I was crying, but later I realized that I had become aware of just how fragile she was. I knew that she could be hurt, that she could become disfigured, that she could get sick, that certainly she would die, and that nothing I could do would keep her safe. I was weeping with anticipated grief, which was an expression of my deepest fears.

Along with a fear of known dangers comes a fear of the unknown. When I pressed one father to explain the urgency of his request that I baptize his son, I had a feeling that something more was at stake than the size of the christening gown. He said, "I don't believe in all this heaven and hell business, but I wouldn't want my child to die without being baptized. I don't really care about getting it done, but I'm afraid not to." The birth of a child may arouse in the most skeptical of people a primitive sense of fear before the mystery of life and death. They may find in their hearts a desire both to acknowledge the fear and to find a source of courage in facing the unknown future for themselves and for their children. Talking about such awesome subjects is more than a little difficult even for religious people so it is no wonder that skeptical people, unable to find the right words to express their fears, talk about the arrival of grandparents and the size of christening gowns.

Longings

Longings are often the mirror image of fears, but they are something more. Wanting to include grandparents and a family christening gown in the ritual centered around the birth of a child may indicate a longing for continuity in a world that seems to have no direction. Making a connection with the past is a way of expressing hope for the future. Taking care of the roots is the only way to assure vigorous growth in the newest branches. The interest in affirming family continuity at the birth of a child may also be an expression of longing for continuity at a deeper or spiritual level. Skeptical people may sense, without putting what they feel into words, that baptism will link their child with a past that extends beyond family memory. Through baptism the child will acquire adopted ancestors in ancient Britain, in the Palestine of Jesus, and in the kingdom of David and Solomon.

Closely related to the longing for continuity is the longing for community. Couples with small children often feel very much alone in their responsibility. For single parents the loneliness may be even more acute. Although skeptical parents may resist getting involved with a church, the very act of bringing a child to what they know is an initiation into a community is an expression of their desire to be connected with other people and to have such connections for their offspring.

Some of the longings reflect areas of life in which the parents themselves have been disappointed; they hope their children will find what they missed. One mother, when I asked what she most wanted for her baby, answered without hesitation, "Self-confidence and a purpose in life." I inquired if these were things she had found for herself. Immediately her face clouded, and she answered in a small voice, "No, but that's what I want for my daughter." For this particular mother, baptism was a ritual expression of her hope than her daughter would find a secret that had always eluded her.

When a child is born, parents may have many expectations that they cannot express but that fill them with joy. Sometimes the desire for baptism surrounded by family and friends is simply a request for an appropriate and time-honored form of celebration. Just having a party and drinking a toast to the new baby cannot express all the joy that is present with a new birth. As with a marriage, a real celebration requires a recognizable ritual form.

Parents

Not all practicing Christians would agree, but I think that even parents with no religious beliefs whatsoever may have legitimate reasons for wanting to have their children baptized. If skeptical parents can acknowledge their deepest fears and longings, they can enter the ritual with integrity. The ritual is primarily for them rather than for the baby, who will have no memory of the event, in much the same way as a funeral is for the mourners and not for the person whose body lies in the casket.

Not all church people think that baptism is primarily for the benefit of parents. Some Christians believe that in baptism a baby is indelibly marked, albeit in an invisible manner. That mark may produce no observable effects but it will assure the child a place in heaven. Skeptics may want to dismiss such people with the taunt that believers use baptism as a way of obtaining "hell insurance" for their children, but to do so would be a mistake. Believers just have their own way of covering up their fears and their longings, a way that on close examination is not so very different from the ones used by skeptics. To argue about whose cover-up is better or worse would be a waste of time.

Skeptics who decide to baptize their children may also have to deal with Christians among their acquaintances who are opposed to infant baptism and who think that the ritual should be reserved for adults who can make a mature affirmation of faith. Arguing with these people is probably not a good idea, either, but skeptics should know the rationale for baptizing babies. In the first place, the practice may be biblical. When, for example, Paul and Silas baptized their jailer "with all his family" at Philippi (Acts 16:33), they gave no indication that they had refused to baptize the children. In the second place, although adult baptism may have been more the norm in the early years of the church, the baptism of small children has been a part of the clearly established tradition of the church since at least the fourth century. In the third place, in rejecting infant baptism, along with all of the other traditions that had evolved in the millennium and a half since the time of the apostles, some sixteenth-century reformers left their followers with no suitable rite of passage to celebrate the birth of a child and to mark the arrival of a new member in the family and in the church.

Adults who were not baptized as children, however, may choose to be baptized in the Episcopal Church. They would use much the same ritual form that parents follow in having their children baptized, but the purpose would be quite different. Adults being baptized are making a public affirmation of faith and accepting responsibility as full members of a Christian community. Parents presenting children for baptism are engaging instead in a rite of passage, celebrating the birth of a child, and acknowledging their need for support in fulfilling their obligations toward their children and society.

Godparents

Christians have always thought that child rearing was too important to be left entirely in the hands of parents. The community as a whole takes responsibility for the nurture of their younger members, but certain adults agree to assist the parents of particular children. Godparents, as these individuals came to be called, in former times occasionally took on the primary task of child rearing. Parents chose them because of their reputations for goodness and wisdom. Today godparents can still play a significant role in the development of a child if they take their promises seriously, because children need adults who are genuinely interested in them.

A teen-aged girl taught me about the importance of children having adult friends. She said, "When something's bothering me, I have a neighbor I talk with. I can't talk about certain things with my mother. She has too much at stake in the way I turn out." Exactly. Parents have too much investment in their children to have much objectivity in sensitive areas, yet the children still need the perspective that only adults can provide. A godparent who maintains an active interest in a child during the early years may develop the kind of trusting relationship that will make useful conversation possible when the child reaches the time of troubling decisions.

No prescription is available for godparents who want to learn how to establish a relationship with their godchildren. Individuals, adults and children alike, are too different to make generalizations very helpful. The most that can be said is that the godparent will have to work at keeping in touch with, and making time for, the godchild. When that happens, the results will be obvious. The godfather of my youngest child was particularly attentive. Each Christmas, even when she was quite small, he would come over and spend an hour or so with her. I have no idea what they talked about, and I was not aware that a bond had formed between them until the day my youngest was with me at the airport. She had recently learned to read, and as we stood waiting for her grandparents to arrive, she puzzled out letters on the sign announcing a major renovation of the facilities for United Airlines. When she got to the last line, listing the name of the architect, she suddenly shouted, "My godfather! That's my godfather's name!" Listening to her delighted shouts and watching her jump up and down with excitement, I knew that my wife and I had chosen the right person for her, a person who had already made a difference in the life of this six-year-old girl.

The parents and godparents assume joint responsibility for seeing that the children learn something about their Christian heritage and participate in a Christian community. That is not a bad idea from the perspective of either the adults or the children. Skeptical parents who want to be extremely pragmatic about child rearing can avail themselves of scientific studies showing that children who grow up in a family with ties to a religious community are less likely to have physical and emotional problems than those who have no experience in a congregation. They develop a stronger sense of identity and self-worth, and as a result, they are less likely to be taken in by cult leaders and drug dealers. As adults they are likely to cope better with the stresses of employment and unemployment, with sickness and with death.

The godparents also join the parents in promising to pray for the children. Skeptical people often have trouble with praying, but they can honor their promise to pray for a child by a simple and useful exercise. They can pause on a regular schedule, once a day or even once a week, and hold the child in mind. They do not have to ask for anything or give thanks for anything, if that seems awkward. They do not even have to concentrate on having any particular thoughts about the child. Holding the child in mind for a few moments will be enough to make them sensitive to the child as a person with particular gifts and special needs.

Perhaps the most important function of a godparent is to be a "witness" for the child. Everybody knows that children learn more from the example adults set for them than by the words adults use in trying to teach them. At the baptism service, the parents and godparents promise to use the power of their witnessing in a conscious and positive way, but the words of the response indicate a recognition of how difficult being a positive witness can be: "I will, with God's help."

Renunciations and Affirmations

The promises the parents and godparents make in the name of a child they present for baptism reveal the Christian view of what constitutes a healthy life. Using symbolic language, they renounce those human tendencies that lead to an unhealthy and unproductive life and affirm the possibilities that lead to a satisfying and rewarding life.

Satan

The promises begin with a renunciation of "Satan". This is a Hebrew word meaning "adversary" or "accuser". In ancient Jewish mythology Satan was not originally associated with the forces of wickedness that rebel against God. Satan played a positive and supportive role as the prosecutor in the heavenly court. The early chapters in the book "Job", however, suggest a significant development in the Satan myth. The accuser makes a false accusation. He becomes a slanderer, the adversary not of God's enemies but of a faithful person. The evolution of the Satan myth reflects a profound understanding of a common human failing: to accept the negative judgments of other people and to prove the accuracy of their assessments by anti-social behavior.

Children in trouble with school authorities or with the law frequently manifest this syndrome. One such teenager was a boy whom I shall call Edmund. Edmund's mother brought him to my office because he had been getting into trouble. Edmund had been skipping school. Edmund had failed two courses in the past year. Now Edmund was in trouble with the police. He had stolen money out of the lockers of his classmates at school. Edmund appeared to be a rather nice boy, shy perhaps, but pleasant. He did not talk much, but when he spoke most of what he said was a variation on the theme, "I guess I'm just no good." At first I wondered how he had come to that conclusion, but I did not have to wonder long after I became acquainted with Edmund's family. From the time he was quite small he had been told, "You're a naughty boy. You never do what you are supposed to do." Edmund had fallen into Satan's trap. He had accepted the verdict of his accusers. Edmund had also found power in being no good, the power to torment his accusers. By skipping school he could shame his parents in the presence of the principal. By failing courses he could embarrass his parents in conferences with his teachers. Edmund finally discovered that he had the power to produce the ultimate humiliation for his parents: he forced them into confrontations with the police sergeant, the juvenile judge, and the probation officer.

Edmund had power, but not the power to get what he really wanted. He wanted to be loved. As I got to know Edmund, I learned that he wanted to be loved by his classmates and his teachers, but most of all he wanted to be loved by his parents. Edmund could not say it in so many words, but what he hungered for was the love of God that could be expressed through the people around him. By accepting the verdict of his accusers, however, Edmund rebelled against God. That is, he made himself all but impossible to love.

Self-deprecation is an ever-present danger in the life of a child. By renouncing Satan, the parents and godparents are promising to treat the child in a way that will allow the child to feel like a person of genuine worth, a person worth loving.

Closely related to the Satan myth is the concept of evil. In fact, Satan is often called simply the Evil One. The way the questions to the parents and godparents are phrased, however, the prayer book is making a distinction between "Satan and all the spiritual forces of wickedness" and "the evil powers of this world". The former suggests internal, psychological pressures, while the latter points to the external threat posed by political and economic systems. Edmund was exposed to both kinds of dangers, and he became a victim of both.

Sin

As the children grow up, they will develop responses to the internal forces symbolized by Satan and the external powers identified as evil. The responses to these hazards of life, which they learn from the adults around them, will determine the kind of life they make for themselves. The responses that make a difficult situation more miserable, the Bible calls "sin". The word that appears as "sin" in English translations of the New Testament stands for a Greek word originally associated with archery, *hamartia*. It means "the arrow fell short of the target".

When the metaphor of being "off-target" is applied to human life, it suggests that responses to certain situations will not lead people to their intended goals. Edmund wanted to be loved and accepted, but his behavior made reaching that goal all but impossible. Using the expression in its original sense, you could say that his responses to the pressures on him "missed the mark", or that they were "sinful".

Sinful behavior as a rule results from sinful desires. I do not mean that people actually desire to miss the mark, but they allow their intention of being on-target to be overridden by a desire to avoid anxiety or despair. To relieve this condition of helplessness and hopelessness, Edmund desired power over other people. In exercising power he may have found some relief from anxiety and despair, but he failed to get what he really wanted. That is the nature of sinful desires. They draw people away from the love of God that they might have found in other people.

Parents and godparents who renounce sinful desires take on the responsibility for helping the children learn to be direct in their dealings with the pressures of life. They are promising to help the children discover that avoiding or denying their responsibilities in order to ease their feelings of anxiety and despair will cause them to fall short of their goals.

Savior

Anyone who has tried to deal directly with anxiety and despair, however, knows that such a stance toward trouble takes more than just grit and determination. That is why at this point in the ritual the promises shift from renunciations to the affirmation of a need for a "savior". To speak of a savior is to make the assumption that you need help in coping with a dangerous or troublesome situation. People who cannot make this assumption, but who believe that they can manage anything all alone, are setting themselves up for disaster.

A young obstetrician, the mother of four small girls, was working long hours as she developed a practice with one other partner. She enjoyed her work and loved her family, but the pressures at home were intense. Her third child, who was just of school age, was manifesting severe learning disabilities, and because of a sudden rise in the mortgage interest rates, her husband's home-building business was on the verge of bankruptcy. Always a heavy drinker, her husband had recently increased his consumption of alcohol at an alarming rate. She was on the verge of collapse, but when she talked about her situation, she insisted that she should be able to meet the needs of all her patients, provide the appropriate kind of nurturing for her daughters, including the disabled child, and prop up her distraught and alcoholic husband.

The obstetrician took some time to discover that she had two problems, one situational and one spiritual. With her high intelligence and analytical mind, she had a good understanding of her situation, but she was spiritually naive. She was not even aware of her own arrogance in assuming that she should be able to take care of all the significant people in her life. Finally, on the advice of a friend she attended an Al-Anon meeting. She heard the spouses of other alcoholics talk about being powerless over alcohol and turning their lives over to a higher power. On reflection, she decided that she was also powerless over her child's malfunctioning neurological system and the capricious movements of the economy that were wrecking her husband's business. Reluctantly, she came to the conclusion that she did need the help of a "higher power". For her the higher power could not be an abstraction, an oblong blur, but needed to have form and substance. Having grown up as a Christian, she decided to let Jesus be the symbolic form for the higher power in her life. With that decision she discovered what it meant to have a savior. The more she learned about Jesus, the more convinced she became that she needed to be saved from her arrogance as well as from her anxiety and despair. When she visualized Jesus Christ as the savior, she saw that she would not be rescued from her situation but would find the strength to do what was possible within her circumstances, without wasting her energy on what was beyond her control.

In one way I sometimes think that families with alcohol problems are the fortunate ones, at least those who follow the twelve steps of Alcoholics Anonymous. They know what it means to need a savior. Other people, with less dramatic or well-defined trouble, often let their arrogance destroy them and their families.

When parents and godparents make the promise to accept Jesus Christ as the Savior, they are promising to create an atmosphere for the children in which the children know it is not shameful to ask for help. They are taking on the responsibility for assisting the children in making realistic self-assessments and in accepting their limits. In the baptism ritual they are also acknowledging their need for help as they ask all the members of the congregation to join them in accepting responsibility for the children. The parents are not alone with the awesome task of rearing children. If they can accept the support, they will be surrounded by a community that will help to sustain them and their children throughout the years.

The Baptismal Covenant

The Baptismal Covenant has something in common with the sort of contracts that are called "covenants" by lawyers and real estate brokers. A legal covenant is a binding agreement between two or more persons or parties. The Baptismal Covenant binds together members of the church with each other and with God. It begins with a primitive form of the creed in a question-and-answer format. The creed in the baptism service is usually referred to as the Apostles' Creed, not to suggest that the original apostles of Jesus wrote it, but to indicate that it represents their teaching and tradition. It probably evolved naturally through the practice of new Christians declaring at the time of their baptism the trust in God that they had developed through Jesus. Skeptics who have trouble with the creed in any form can turn to the chapter on the Nicene Creed in section two, "Getting Past the Barriers".

Then the liturgy continues with five more questions. The first is based on a statement in the Acts of the Apostles (2:42) describing life in the first Christian community, which the disciples of Jesus organized in Jerusalem. The others are of more recent origin: "Will you continue in the apostles' teaching and fellowship, in the breaking of bread, and in the prayers?"

By promising to continue in the apostles' teaching, the parents and godparents are saying that they will see to it that the children learn about the Christian tradition. If not from a religious standpoint, at least from an intellectual one, children deserve to know something about their heritage and the origins of western culture.

The biblical word "fellowship" could also be translated "community" or "partnership". The root of the word in Greek is a verb meaning "to share". Children need the experience of participating in a community where they can see authority and responsibility being shared among people who care about each other.

The breaking of bread and the prayers are the two principal acts of Christian worship: the Eucharist and common prayer. To feel that they belong to the community, children need the experience of worship with adults. Inviting youngsters to share in the broken bread at Holy Communion is a practice re-introduced to the Episcopal Church within recent memory. For centuries children were excluded unless they had made a mature affirmation of faith and had been confirmed, something that usually took place as they entered their teen-age years. When the church finally abandoned the ritual rejection of children at communion, the prevailing attitude was that the children should never be able to remember a time when they were not welcome at the Lord's table.

"Will you persevere in resisting evil, and, whenever you fall into sin, repent and return to the Lord?" Notice that the expression is not *if* you fall into sin, but *whenever*. Human beings appear to have a natural proclivity for side-stepping and evading responsibility and for denying and avoiding what causes anxiety or despair. People who are determined to live the kind of life described in baptism are not going to be sinless, but they will be freed from the necessity of always responding to pressure in ways that "miss the mark".

The New Testament word "repent" means "turn". To switch the metaphor from archery to sailing, you can think of life as a voyage against the current and into the wind. You get set on what appears to be the correct course, but then you discover that if you do not change your direction you will surely go aground. Then as you are comfortably settled on a new tack, you notice that the wind has shifted or that you are approaching the rocks on the opposite shore, and you have to change direction again. A willingness to repent is something like tacking: trying to do the best you can but changing direction as soon as you discover you are making a mess out of your life.

Will you proclaim by word and example the Good News of God in Christ? "Good News" is the literal meaning of "gospel". If the children being baptized choose the life their parents and godparents intend for them, their presence will be good news to the people among whom they will live and work. By the way they talk and behave, they will demonstrate to other people that they have adopted a way of life in which they are sustained in joy and upheld through tragedy. For them Christianity will not be oppressive or coercive, but freeing and challenging. The Christian way of life will be good news to the children as they are growing up and good news to the people who get to know them. Will you seek and serve Christ in all persons, loving your neighbor as yourself? Will you strive for justice and peace among all people, and respect the dignity of every human being?

One way to avoid any sense of responsibility for other human beings who disgust or threaten us is to decide that they are less than human. When I was a child, I asked a World War II veteran of the Pacific Theater what it was like to kill people. He responding by saying, "Shooting Japs wasn't like killing people. We were just picking off monkeys in the trees." I have heard white people deny any social responsibility for poor inner-city Blacks by insisting, "They are just a bunch of animals." The promise in baptism is not only to see such people as fellow human beings, but to recognize the divine presence in them and to respond accordingly. This promise does not tell you what to do in time of war or social dislocation, but if the children being baptized learn to follow the intention of the promise, they will not try to escape from responsibility by denying the humanity of other people.

Thanksgiving over the Water

After the Prayers for the Candidates, the focus of the ritual moves to the water. In most Episcopal churches the water will have been poured into a basin supported by a pedestal of stone, metal, or wood. The whole structure is called a "font", a word from the same root as "fountain" and with a similar meaning: a spring or a source of water. The prayer points to some of the ancient symbolic connections people have made with water.

> We thank you, Almighty God, for the gift of water. Over it the Holy Spirit moved at the beginning of creation. Through it you led the children of Israel out of their bondage in Egypt into the land of promise. In it your son Jesus received the baptism of John and was anointed by the Holy Spirit as the Messiah, the Christ, to lead us, through his death and resurrection, from the bondage of sin into everlasting life.
>
> We thank you, Father, for the water of Baptism. In it we are buried with Christ in his death. By it we share in his resurrection. Through it we are reborn by the Holy Spirit. Therefore in joyful obedience to your Son, we bring into his fellowship those who come to him in faith, baptizing them in the Name of the Father, and of the Son, and of the Holy Spirit.
>
> Now sanctify this water, we pray you, by the power of your Holy Spirit, that those who here are cleansed from sin and

born again may continue for ever in the risen life of Jesus Christ our Savior.

"In the beginning," we read in the Book of Genesis, "the earth was without form and void, and darkness was upon the face of the deep; and the Spirit of God was moving over the face of the waters" (Genesis 1:1-2). Water—as it appears in the raging of the seas and the devastation of the floods—is the symbol of chaos. Water is the reminder of the fragile nature of the structures we invent in order to keep the chaos at bay.

Water is also the symbol of life. The human embryo develops in water. Water brings life to all plants as well as animals. Rain and the melting snow nourish the earth. Expanding the metaphor, we can think of a particular quality of life as an ever-flowing stream from which we can drink. Being led to everlasting life does not necessarily mean that we are guaranteed continued self-conscious existence after we die, but rather may suggest that we can participate in a quality of life that can best be described as eternal or everlasting because that quality has always been available and always will be.

Although water represents life, it is a reminder of death and burial as well. In baptism, the child is "buried with Christ in his death." In facing death and in dying, Jesus entered the experience of every human being: the father weeping with anticipated grief for his infant daughter, the teenager who stole because he did not know how to ask for love. In baptizing children, we symbolically identify them with Christ's death in the hope that when they enter the chaos, they will find they are not alone, but that God was there before them waiting to uphold and sustain them.

I knew an attorney whose life was given shape during the seven exhausting years she spent in the service of a distinguished law firm as she tried to prove herself worthy of becoming a partner. When the time came, she was not accepted, and she felt as if she were drowning, the waters of chaos closing over her head. Then she discovered something else, the strength to accept her disappointment and anger and the courage to chart a new course for herself serving the public interest in a government agency. As a result of this first failure in her life, she found that she no longer looked with contempt on those who did not measure up to her standards of success;

she possessed a new sensitivity to other people, both in their joy and in their pain.

Through water the child is said to be reborn. "Reborn" and "born again" are both somewhat inadequate translations for the New Testament words *gennao anothen*, a Greek phrase with a double meaning used in the third chapter of the Gospel according to St. John to illustrate the foolishness of taking religious language as if it were describing objective reality. In this story Jesus uses the word to tell his visitor, Nicodemus, what he must do to enter the kingdom of God. In obvious astonishment, Nicodemus asks, "How can a man be born when he is old? Can he enter a second time into his mother's womb and be born?" The exchange between Nicodemus and Jesus is based on the double meaning of the adverb, *anothen*, which can indicate either the repetition of a process or a new dimension, in this case literally "from above". In the story, Jesus is obviously using the word in a metaphorical sense, pointing to the necessity of Nicodemus finding a new dimension to his life, which—to continue with a spatial metaphor— may have been flat or narrow.

Another common use of water is to make clean what was soiled. Since long before the dawn of history human beings have used water to wash their dirty bodies, their dirty clothes, and their dirty utensils. It is not surprising that they used water in a ritual when they felt contaminated by moral or religious failure. It was probably this custom of ritual cleansing before worship that gave rise to the requirement that Gentiles seeking access to Judaism be baptized. John the Baptist's insistence that Jews themselves needed to be baptized may have drawn on both the custom of ritual washing before worship and the admission of new converts to Judaism. Both had to do with the removal of moral stain in preparation for a fresh beginning.

The Baptism
At this point in the liturgy of baptism, the actions speak more loudly than the words. The parents present the children to the celebrants; they voluntarily give them up. In so doing they remind themselves that if they fulfill their responsibility to nurture their children, the children will grow up and leave

them. The point of the nurturing is to prepare the children for life outside of the family and away from their parents.

The celebrants then perform three ritual acts with each child. In the first, a priest or deacon immerses each child in the water or pours water over each child's head. The children are symbolically put to death; they are abandoned to the waters of chaos. In this act the parents are reminded of the conflicting feelings they will have about their children. "I was so mad I could have killed them" is not an uncommon reaction in exasperating moments, such as finding your children in their best clothes all covered with mud just minutes before you are scheduled to leave for the church to attend your sister's wedding. At the same time the worst fear most parents have is that they will experience the death of a child.

Each child is raised up from the symbolic death with a name. The name indicates that the child is a person, not just an extension of the parents. The child was born with a family name, but this name was chosen just for this child. Here is somebody in particular, somebody special. In giving the child a name, the parents declare that they recognize this person as a unique individual. In the future they will do well to remember their grammar when they refer to "our child". The pronoun in the genitive case does not necessarily indicate actual possession but may refer to another kind of relationship. We can see the U.S. flag waving over the capitol and say honestly and proudly, "That is our flag," knowing full well that the flag belongs to the Congress. In the same fashion, parents need to remind themselves that their children do not belong to them.

Then one of the celebrants performs the second ritual act, the chrism. The ancient custom of anointing the newly-baptized Christians with oil blessed by the bishop has recently been revived in the Episcopal Church. The act not only identifies the person with Christ, literally "the anointed one", but reminds the parents of the purposes for which people were anointed with oil in biblical times. Oil was used not only for cosmetic and medicinal purposes, but also in the ritual granting of authority. When the prophet Samuel declared that the young shepherd David was to be the king of Israel, he "took the horn of oil, and anointed him in the midst of his brothers; and the Spirit of the Lord came mightily upon David from that time forward" (I Samuel 10:13). When they see their children anointed, parents may realize that these infants will be special people with important tasks to perform and that they will need the help of their mothers and fathers in growing up with a sense of being significant. The chrism represents the way provided parents to help their children resist the human tendencies symbolized by Satan, the false accuser. Instead of allowing their children to think of themselves as bad or worthless, the parents will bring their children up to see themselves as attractive, healthy, valuable people.

The parents will also notice that the celebrant applies the oil in the shape of a cross: the instrument of torture and death, the sign of ultimate tragedy. In order to discover and carry out their assignment in this world, the children must face agony and turmoil and finally death. This act will remind the parents that tragedy and joy, as well as success and failure, are inseparable in the scheme of things and that they must help their children learn to face the whole of reality in finding their unique places in the universe.

In the first two ritual acts, each child is declared a special individual with a unique calling. The third act, the reception into "the household of God," reminds the parents of a paradox: their children can only discover their individuality and uniqueness in relationship with other people. One purpose of "the household of God" is to help people of all ages identify and develop their gifts and talents so that their lives can be more satisfying and so that they will have more to offer for the common good. Becoming both an individual and a responsible member of a community will, however, present the children and their parents with an eternal tension. That tension may be identified at church, but it will be present in the family as well and frequently confront the parents with a painful dilemma.

To introduce new parents to the kind of dilemmas they will face as their children grow older, I have often presented them with the case of a teenager whose uninvited guests—all close friends—bring beer to the house when the parents are away, having left strict orders that no alcoholic beverages are permitted. When I ask parents what they would want for their children in such a situation, they normally say that they would want their children to have the strength of their convictions and to stand on their own two feet. When pressed, however, they usually admit that what they mean is they would want the children to have the strength of the parents' convictions and to take a stand against their peers. If the parents succeeded in bringing up the children with such an attitude, the children could never leave home and never function as independent individuals. Yet without the sense of family standards and traditions, the children cannot find an identity that will sustain them in their independence. Giving the child a name at baptism represents one side of the tension—the necessity of being an individual, while receiving the child into the community represents the other side—the necessity of being part of a community. As long as parents can live with their children in this tension, the children will have a chance of emerging from the family as healthy people.

Through symbolic language and ritual acts, the sacrament of baptism can help prepare even skeptical parents for the responsibilities they face in rearing children. Even more important, baptism can point them toward the kind of support they will need in the coming years. Through baptism, parents may enlist the support not only of godparents but of a caring community that understands the fears and longings that are always present in mothers and fathers.

Chapter 8
THE BURIAL OF THE DEAD

Skeptics who have successfully faced each crisis in their lives armed simply with the resources that they have acquired through education and experience may still turn to the church when someone close to them dies. The rituals provided by a religious community offer the best avenue for the recovery from grief. In fact, attempts to face death without the support of traditional forms for grieving can lead to trouble. A comprehensive report on bereavement sponsored by the National Academy of Sciences, the National Academy of Engineering, and the Institute of Medicine contained a warning that the absence of prescribed forms for mourning and bereavement "may result in serious adjustment and recovery problems for the recently bereaved." Their continuing distress may manifest itself in symptoms of mental or physical illness.

A woman in the neighborhood who had seldom attended any church asked her husband to call me because she did not seem to be recovering from her mother's death. Her mother, a remarkably wise and sensitive woman in most respects, had said that she wanted her body to be given to a medical school and did not want a funeral. In attempting to honor her mother's requests, the daughter had deprived herself of the appropriate means for expressing her grief. When she realized that the funeral is not for the sake of the dead but for the bereaved, however, she accepted my offer to conduct a memorial service for the family. We read the order for The Burial of the Dead, and at the place of the homily we talked about her mother. In this gathering, although I had never met the dead woman whose life we were celebrating, I was deeply moved by a sense of her presence among us, especially as the grieving woman's daughters acknowledged how their grandmother had influenced their lives, both directly and through their mother. Their grandmother, although skeptical of the claims made by the church, had manifested the traits which religious people most admire. Crippled since childhood and abandoned by her husband not long after the birth of her daughter, she had found the courage and strength to lead an independent life and to be open and loving to the people around her. Her only obvious failure was that she did not realize how much her daughter would miss her and how much help her daughter would need in recovering from her grief.

Adjusting to the loss of a loved and admired parent may be difficult, but coping with the death of a destructive one can be even worse. One lawyer of my acquaintance was devastated by his mother's death. He had never been able to please his mother during her lifetime, but he was not prepared for the judgment on his life reflected in her will. Of the four children in the family, he was the best qualified by age and profession to be the executor of the estate, but his mother chose a younger sister instead. Setting up the younger children to make him appear to be incompetent or unworthy of trust was an old pattern that he had to face again with her death. His feelings of rejection and rage made his grief harder to bear than it would have been if his primary reaction had been simply loss. The rituals provided by the church, however, which not only gave him permission to be angry but also assured him of his individual worth, helped him to deal with his mother's death and get on with his life.

The basic ritual in the prayer book for coping with bereavement is called "The Burial of the Dead". It is preceded, however, by two other rituals under the heading "Ministration at the Time of Death". Because many people are not aware of the possibilities contained in these two services, I will touch on them briefly before moving on to explore the insights of the burial office itself.

Litany at the Time of Death

Agnes called me just as I was getting ready for bed. Her husband, a wonderful old gentlemen in his mid-nineties, who had been ailing for some time, was dying. As I drove across town to their house, I thought of all he had meant to me over the past twenty years. He had been an old man as long as I had known him, but he had always been a ready source of energy and perspective. Every time I put the communion bread in the those big, gnarled hands and took in his slight smile and merry eyes, I felt somehow uplifted. One of the last times he had made it to church, I had told him how much I had missed him on previous Sundays. "Well," he replied, "it won't be long before I never miss another service. I won't miss a party or a meeting, either. I'm going to be right here." As he spoke, he was pointing to a wall of the church that we had set aside for a columbarium, a place to build niches for receiving the ashes of our church members who have died.

Agnes met me at the door with the news that he had stopped breathing, but she asked me to come up to his room and read with her the litany to be used at the time of death. He looked peaceful, almost radiant in death, but I was filled with a sense of sorrow and of my own inadequacy. Anything I might say to Agnes would sound trite and hollow so I was grateful for her suggestion that we read the litany. My eyes were filled with tears as we neared the end of the prayers. "Depart, O Christian soul, out of this world . . . May your rest be this day in peace, and your dwelling place in the Paradise of God." I cannot claim to know what happens to people when they die, but I do know the sense of comfort that comes with entrusting an old friend to God's care.

You cannot always arrange for people you love to die at a time when you can avail yourself of this ritual form to help you begin the process of grieving, but when you know the end is near, I suggest you keep a copy of The Book of Common Prayer handy with a marker at page 462. When death comes, reading aloud the Litany at the Time of Death, either by yourself or with other people, may help you through the first stage of shock and sorrow.

Prayers for a Vigil

When Jane died, her mother arrived from Boston to take charge of the funeral arrangements. Jane's mother was a Roman Catholic. Although she did not seem to be at all put out that her daughter had been active in an Episcopal Church, she did want to observe old family customs: "We will have a wake, won't we?" I was willing to oblige, but I had to confess that I had never been to a wake and was not sure what we were supposed to do. "Why," she said, "the night before the funeral you just bring food and wine and maybe some other things to drink over to the church, and you sit around and talk about the person who has died. Then you say some prayers. And then you go home."

I was willing to preside at such a gathering, but I felt it needed some structure so I was looking through what was then our newly revised Book of Common Prayer, where I found "Prayers for a Vigil". The prayers seemed to be appropriate, but the ritual was new to me. A little background reading brought me to the conclusion that what the Irish call a wake the English call a vigil. The prayers I found had been put in the prayer book for just the kind of occasion Jane's mother had requested.

As people gathered at the church for the vigil, I noticed that we had at least three distinct groups present who had known Jane but who had never met each other: members of the congregation, her fellow graduate students, and her family. After people had gathered, I asked them to be seated and told them what little I knew about wakes or vigils. I said that sitting in silence would be fine, but if people wanted to talk about Jane, they were free to stand up and speak. The church people were the least bashful. One after another they stood up and told stories about Jane that illustrated what a difficult person she had been. I became increasingly uncomfortable when the comments by the graduate students by and large followed the same theme. At about the time I decided we had heard enough about how headstrong and demanding Jane had been, her brother stood up and introduced himself. I could feel the rustle of embarrassment throughout the room as the church people and the graduate students suddenly became aware that Jane's family might have been offended by all of this blunt talk. Her brother put everyone at ease, however, by announcing, "You think Jane was difficult? You don't know just how difficult she was! I do. I had to live in the same house with her all those years we were growing up."

After the laughter subsided, many of the people who had already spoken, as well as many who had not, confessed that in spite of the aggravation that Jane had caused them, they had held her in great affection and would sorely miss her. Gradually the sense of loss and sorrow came to the surface, and the three separate groups who had known Jane became one in their grief. When the time seemed right, I offered the vigil prayers, and after each the people responded, "Into your hands, O Lord, we commend our sister Jane."

Sometimes family members learn from other people at a vigil that the dead person had qualities they had not perceived. These discoveries can be painful, but also comforting. When George, one of the most respected members of our congregation, died, everyone assumed that we would gather for a vigil the night before the funeral, that is, everyone but the two middle-aged sons who had arrived from distant cities. Neither of the sons had a church affiliation, and both were dubious about "going through the emotional strain of a funeral twice." They agreed to join us, however, and were surprised to find the church packed with people. One by one both men and women stood up to tell stories about how George had been a mentor and friend. Many said that George had been more of a father for them than their own fathers had been. In some ways these testimonials were hard for George's sons to take because when they were young, he had often been emotionally inaccessible or too busy for them. Other people had received from George what they had been denied. At the same time these two grown sons gained a new appreciation of their father. In his retirement following a serious illness, their father had developed a new sensitivity for other people and a new capacity for intimacy. In his advanced age he had acquired wisdom that had drawn younger people to him and had made him the acknowledged patriarch of the community. As George's sons gained an appreciation for what their father had become, they were able to forgive him for what he had not been to them. As they found themselves surrounded by a community of people who had loved their father and were grieving for him, they experienced the comfort available to those who are bound together in grief.

"Blessed are those who mourn"

Skeptics may note that when people participate in the prayer book rituals at the time of death, the comfort they receive does not depend upon believing. People experience comfort when they are willing to acknowledge their grief in the midst of a community that is acquainted with grief. According to the gospels, Jesus observed, "Blessed are those who mourn, for they shall be comforted." That word translated "blessed" actually means "fortunate". The fortunate people are those who are willing to acknowledge their sorrow because they will be strengthened and healed. Just think: two thousand years ago, long before anyone had undertaken a scientific study of bereavement, an itinerant teacher from the little village of Nazareth in Galilee had discovered that human beings need to mourn. Skeptics may also note that Jesus placed no more emphasis on believing than have behavioral scientists. Recovery from bereavement comes through appropriate forms of mourning, not through believing.

In fact, believing can sometimes be a barrier to recovery from bereavement. Christians who firmly believe that the dead are in paradise with God may also believe that death should be a time for rejoicing and that sorrow is a selfish emotion. One woman told me that she did not cry when her infant daughter died because her pastor told her that she should be glad that God had chosen her child to be with him as one of the angels. Years later, after her marriage had failed and after several prolonged bouts of depression, with the help of a psychotherapist she was finally able to weep for her dead child. Jesus had it right. The fortunate people are not those who believe, but those who mourn.

Mourning, however, can be a complicated business. Death stirs up a combination of primitive and powerful emotions that produce the reaction known as grief. In addition to a sense of loss, grief may include anger, guilt, and fear.

When my own father died, I was shocked by the intensity of my grief. I thought I had prepared myself during the two weeks I had spent at his bedside waiting for him to die. As his breathing became more labored, I even prayed that he would give up the struggle, but when at last his breathing stopped and the nurse assured us that his heart was no longer beating, I was overwhelmed with a sense of pain that I had never known before. Through my convulsive sobbing, I could scarcely get out the words of the prayer I wanted to say for my sake as well as the sake of my mother, who was holding his hand on the other side of the bed. In the days that followed as we prepared for the funeral, I was able to sort out my feelings and to understand something about the nature of my grief.

Loss. Until he was gone, I did not realize how much his simply being there had meant to me. I was proud of the fact that he only had to support me for two and a half out of the seven years I had spent in getting an education beyond high school. I seldom asked to borrow money, but I could face the possibility of financial difficulty with confidence because I knew he would be there with funds any time I called on him for help. I had been much more inclined to ask for advice than for money, and he had always been there when I wanted to call on his wisdom and his experience as a lawyer. He had always been there as my link to the past; he had provided me with a sense of continuity, tradition, and identity. Now he was gone. I was simply not prepared to take on my new role as the oldest surviving man in the family.

Anger. I did not realize how angry I was until after he died. I had received a call that he was failing rapidly and would probably not last more than a day or two. I flew home immediately, of course, but I could not help wondering if the timing of his death might force me to cancel my plans to spend two weeks in Israel with a group of parishioners on a tour we had been planning for over a year. By the time I got home, he had rallied slightly, and he stubbornly clung to life long enough for me to miss the trip. Missing my chance to see the Holy Land upset me, but what made me really angry was that the two weeks I sat there waiting for him to die seemed like such a waste. By that time the brain cancer had progressed so far that no communication with him was possible, and I was denied the possibility of a proper deathbed farewell. I was also angry that the doctors had unnecessarily prolonged the agony of his death with their useless surgery and radiation treatments. Finally, as I watched him slowly wasting away, I became angry with God for setting up a system for life that ends in such decay and misery. I could not help thinking that sooner or later this would be my fate as well.

Guilt. Although I had been a reasonably good son and had not given my father too much trouble, I was uneasy about several aspects of my behavior. I do not think I had ever told him how proud I was of his achievements and of the contributions he had made to the town and county in which he had lived for the past fifty years. I had not often returned home for visits but had depended upon my parents coming to see me and my family. During the last two weeks I had prayed for him to die. I had even agreed to increasing his medication for pain in the knowledge that it might quicken his death. Part of my grief was the guilt that arose when I realized how relieved I felt when the end came.

Fear. Both guilt and anger may mask the deeper and more troublesome emotion of fear. Guilt may be the fear of being caught, judged, and punished. Anger may be a defensive reaction to a threat. Part of my grief was in reality my fear of being a failure and my fear of dying.

The Sting of Death

In every experience, the mix and intensity of the emotions will be different from every other; such emotions are not altogether predictable. The mix will depend upon the circumstances, and the intensity will probably be determined by the closeness of the relationship and the timeliness of the death. Losing a child is bound to be harder than losing a parent. Losing a spouse is obviously more painful than losing an old friend of the family.

Suicide is the cause of death likely to produce the most complicated and intense emotions. Not long after I came to my present parish, one of our parish leaders slit her wrists. The coroner's report listed the cause of death as "exsanguination". Her death plunged many members of the congregation into profound grief. With the help of a psychiatrist, we discovered that part of the grief was due to guilt. All of us could recall warning signs, little buzzers sounding within us when we were with her, that should have tipped us off that she was sliding into a depression. We were also suffering from anger. By killing herself she had betrayed everything the church stands for. The intensity of the anger made me think that the church in the middle ages may have had a good reason for adopting what today may seem like a barbaric ritual for burying people who commit suicide. For centuries, when people killed themselves, the mourners could work out their anger by digging a pit at the cross roads, tossing in the body, driving a stake through the heart, filling in the hole, and then tramping and driving across the grave until the suicide was forgotten.

If the intensity of the grief seems out of proportion to the situation, that is a clue that something else is wrong. One young man found himself experiencing convulsions of grief at a funeral for a great-aunt who died when she was nearly ninety. With some help he discovered that the death of the old lady, to whom he had never been very close, had triggered the grief he had never acknowledged but had experienced as a little boy when his mother died and he had been sent away to live with his grandparents. For all his life until that funeral for the old great-aunt, the stored-up grief had sapped his emotional energy and had poisoned his relationships, especially with women.

St. Paul apparently knew about the destructive results observable in the lives of people who are not able to acknowledge the full extent of their grief. In writing to the Christians at Corinth, he asked a rhetorical question, "O death, where is thy sting?" The question he raised was not what makes death painful, but what gives death its venomous power to poison all of life? In the letter, St. Paul immediately answers his own question: "The sting of death is sin." Here is that critical word again, in Paul's language, *hamartia*, which means that "the arrow missed the mark." People do not recover from an encounter with death when their responses are "off the mark", that is, when they do not go straight to the emotions that constitute grief and deal with them. When people avoid, deny, or cover up grief they make healing difficult, if not impossible.

The Burial of the Dead

The burial service in the prayer book can help give bereaved people, including skeptics, both the permission and the confidence they need to grieve. The Book of Common Prayer includes two versions of The Burial of the Dead. Rite One uses language from the time of Queen Elizabeth I and Rite Two employs more modern forms, eliminating archaic verb endings as well as "thee" and "thou". The choice belongs to the bereaved family, but I have noticed that people who have had no church contact for years almost always choose Rite One. Apparently the dignified cadences and poetic tones of Elizabethan English call them back to the security of childhood and the certainty of simpler times. Frankly, I feel the same way. For most worship I prefer the contemporary forms, but at a funeral the ancient language has a strong appeal. Perhaps because the forms are not those of ordinary speech, I am less likely to be troubled by uncongenial ideas and more likely to find meaning on a deeper level.

No matter how overcome with sorrow I may be as I wait to begin a funeral for a close friend, I find my confidence returning as we begin with the words:

> I am the resurrection and the life, saith the Lord; he that believeth in me, though he were dead, yet shall he live; and whosoever liveth and believeth in me shall never die. I know that my Redeemer liveth, and that he shall stand at the latter day upon the earth; and though this body be destroyed, yet shall I see God; whom I shall see for myself and mine eyes shall behold, and not as a stranger.

Believers who have gathered to bury a fellow believer may find consolation from the opening sentence because it appears to claim that the one who has died is not really dead, but alive in Christ.

Skeptics, however, may also find consolation from the same words by taking a different approach. They may recall that the burial service is addressed to them, not to the person whose body is in the coffin. The mourners who are weighed down with sorrow may hear the promise that when they have passed through this experience of death they will be lifted up. Believing in the Lord for a skeptic may mean expressing confidence in a source of courage and healing that will make possible a recovery from grief.

Skeptics who have difficulty in accepting this kind of believing as legitimate may need to consult the Gospel according to St. John, which is the only place in the Bible that includes the words of the first sentence of the burial service and attributes them to Jesus. The author of this gospel warns the reader several times that the words are not to be taken in their literal or objective sense, but are to be understood metaphorically or symbolically. One of these warnings occurs in the exchange between Jesus and his friend Martha in chapter eleven, from which the opening sentence is taken. Martha, speaking of her dead brother, says to Jesus, "I know that he will rise again in the resurrection at the last day." Jesus responds, "I am the resurrection." What is the author doing here? Resurrection in the normal sense of the word refers to an event, but in this story Jesus tells Martha that she has it all wrong. Resurrection is not a future event, but a person. Jesus challenges her conventional way of thinking about resurrection by telling her that through him she may, in that moment, experience resurrection—be raised up from the depths of her grief. As long as she clings to the notion that it is something that only happens to people after they are dead and buried, she will miss the point: resurrection is always a present possibility.

In much the same way that the first sentence assures people they can dare to feel as awful as they do, because they will be lifted out of the depths of their grief, the second sentence gives people permission to experience the full complexity of the feelings that constitute their grief.

The quotation, which comes from the nineteenth chapter of Job, may have special meaning for skeptics when they understand the context. These particular words of Job appear near the end of a speech in which he angrily rejects the attempts of his religious friends to comfort him by finding explanations for his misery. In this same speech Job also directs his anger toward God:

> He has walled up my way, so that I cannot pass,
> and he has set darkness upon my paths.
> He has stripped from me my glory,
> and has taken the crown from my head.
> He breaks me down on every side, and I am gone,
> and my hope he has pulled up like a tree.
> He has kindled his wrath against me,
> and counts me as his adversary.
> His troops come on together;
> they have cast up siegeworks against me,
> and encamp round about my tent.
> He has put my brethren far from me,
> and my acquaintances are wholly estranged from me.

Although Job correctly refuses to accept guilt for the death of his children and the loss of all that was dear to him, he willingly mourns the loss and openly pours out his anger as well as his fear. His assertion that he will find a redeemer who will vindicate him is an expression of defiance aimed both at his religious friends and at God. "I will see God" is not a pious claim, but Job's outraged demand that God give an accounting for the way God has treated him.

During the reading of these two sentences and other brief quotations from the Bible, the family and closest friends of the person who has died customarily follow the clergy into the church carrying the coffin, or the urn of ashes, which they place before the altar steps. Then all take their places for the first prayer.

At the Burial of a Child

One of two options for the first prayer is for use at the burial of a child. Whenever I notice this prayer, I feel a slight twinge of pain in my chest. I think of my three daughters, all alive and well in their twenties, and I cannot imagine anything worse than one of them dying. I have been with people who have lost children, and I have seen the terrible agony that they must endure.

One Friday evening, just as we sat down with guests for dinner, I received a telephone call that the teenaged son of a widow had just died in a boating accident. No one was quite sure what he was doing out on the lake in a small rowboat just at dusk, or how it happened to capsize, or why he could not have managed to swim the scant fifty yards to the shore. The only indisputable fact was that the boy had drowned. When I arrived, I found some neighbors trying to comfort the grieving mother by telling her that the good die young because God needs them in heaven. Such talk did little to relieve her suffering since she knew perfectly well that her son was not a particularly good boy; he had been experimenting with alcohol and other drugs and getting a reputation as a trouble-maker at school. She had loved him dearly, however, and had not given up hope that he would straighten out. So what could people say that might ease the pain in her heart? In my opinion, that is the wrong question to ask under such circumstances. Trying to ease her pain was a mistake. The reason her neighbors were trying so hard was not so much for her sake as for their own. They were, quite naturally, trying to make some sense out of this tragedy and trying to deal with their fears for their own children.

What proved to be more help to the grieving mother was encouragement to talk about her real feelings toward God, her rage and bewilderment. The real question for her was how could she take the body of her dead son into a church and pray to a god who had let him die? She thought that she could never pray again, until the words of the prayer book reminded her that the prayers in the burial service are addressed to one who lost a son, an only child whose tragic death has never been satisfactorily explained. In some of her renewed attempts at prayer, she found that she could pour out her grief because she felt she was praying to one who would understand. In time, she found that the people who were the most comfort to her were other parents who had lost children, but this same principle continued to work in her prayers. What helps to recover from grief is not an explanation for the tragedy, but the confidence of being understood.

Passages from Holy Scripture

After the initial prayer, the burial service offers lessons and psalms from the Bible. Sometimes reading through the suggestions listed in the prayer book and making selections for the funeral can itself be part of the healing process for the bereaved. They may find some encouragement in discovering that for at least two or three thousand years people have gone through grief similar to their own.

Many, including skeptics, find that the psalms are especially helpful. The words put down by these Hebrew poets in ancient times often express what grief-stricken people are feeling but are unable to put into their own words. The psalms continue with what was begun in the opening sentences of the burial service: they give the mourners both the permission and the confidence they need to grieve. One allows those in grief to admit they have a quarrel with God: "O let thine ears consider well the voice of my complaint." Another recognizes that God may not seem to be around when most needed: "O hide not thou thy face from me." The intensity of grief is compared to being overwhelmed by a storm at sea or on a mountainside: "the waters thereof rage and swell . . . and the mountains shake at the tempest." The symptoms of grief are acknowledged: "My tears have been my meat day and night." Guilt also finds a place: "Thou hast set our misdeeds before thee, and our secret sins in the light of thy countenance." An awareness of each person's mortality, perhaps even each person's fear of death, is included: "Though men be so strong that they come to fourscore years, yet is their strength then but labor and sorrow, so soon passeth it away, and we are gone."

Besides allowing people in grief to express their pain, the psalms give them a way of articulating their longing for God to relieve them of that pain. In times of grief, skeptics may not be able to assert any confidence in God, but they may recognize a kindred spirit in the psalmist who wrote: "My soul is athirst for God, yea, even for the living God." Skeptics may even find some help from the psalms that clearly state a trust in God. If those statements are heard as expressions of longing rather than as factual claims, the words can also assist mourners in becoming honest with themselves about their desire for comfort and for healing:

God is our hope and strength,
a very present help in trouble. (Ps. 46)

Lord, thou hast been our refuge,
from one generation to another. (Ps. 90)

My help cometh even from the Lord,
who hath made heaven and earth. (Ps. 121)

Yea, though I walk through the valley of the shadow of death,
I will fear no evil;
for thou art with me;
thy rod and thy staff, they comfort me. (Ps. 23)

Along with the psalms, which the members of the congregation usually read together, the prayer book suggests lessons from the Bible for people to hear. In going over the list of possible readings from the Hebrew Scriptures, skeptics may find that they are a little too heavy on theological reassurance to be of real comfort, especially if the funeral is for someone who was not a practicing Jew or Christian. For that reason, I have frequently suggested on such occasions a reading from the Bible's own skeptic, who is known in Hebrew as "Qoheleth". The teachings of Qoheleth, probably a Jerusalem schoolmaster in the late fourth or early third century BCE, are preserved in the book Ecclesiastes. Many people without orthodox religious convictions have found a promise of healing in the third chapter, a poem that is rendered in the New English Bible, "For everything its season, and for every activity under heaven its time":

> a time to be born and a time to die;
> a time to plant and a time to uproot;
> a time to kill and a time to heal;
> a time to pull down and a time to build up;
> a time to weep and a time to laugh.

I think the passage is especially useful if the reader continues on for a few lines after the end of the poem: "I have seen the business that God has given [human beings] to keep them busy. He has made everything to suit its time; moreover he has given [human beings] a sense of time past and future, but no comprehension of God's work from beginning to end." Some skeptics find real encouragement in discovering that the Bible includes the observations of an authority whose opinions agree with their own. In the face of death, human beings cannot comprehend the meaning of death or of life, but they can see that somehow life goes on. The funeral is a time of death and weeping, but a time will come when they will know healing and laughter.

One of the suggestions in the burial service for a New Testament reading often makes sense to skeptics who have had a chance to think about what the selection actually says. I am speaking of the "sting of death" passage in the fifteenth chapter of St. Paul's first letter to the Corinthians. The passage states bluntly, "The last enemy to be destroyed is death." No sugar coating for a bitter pill found here. Death is not passively accepted as part of the natural rhythm of nature to be embraced without protest. Death is the enemy. Death inflicts pain. Death robs life of meaning. To pretend otherwise conditions people to deny their reactions to death and to subject themselves to death's sting. Because the corrosive power of death comes through sin, through side-stepping and evasion, one way to defeat the power of death is to confront the enemy directly by facing the reality of loss, anger, guilt, and fear.

Doing battle with the power of death is a frightening and wearing business. Maybe that is why many skeptics respond positively to the words attributed to Jesus in the passage from the fourteenth chapter of the Gospel according to St. John, which is also one of the suggested readings: "In my Father's house are many rooms; if it were not so, would I have told you that I go to prepare a place for you?" The kind of house envisioned here is like a four-room Victorian cottage that was planned to grow with an expanding family. A porch is enclosed to make a new room for the second child, and a new porch added, which will in turn be enclosed to build a study. An addition can be put on to accommodate a married daughter and her husband who is in medical school. The house always has room. This organic understanding of living space was also part of the culture in which Jesus grew up. I have seen excavations of houses in Galilee that clearly developed according to this pattern. They had grown to make room for the people who needed to live there. The gospel passage helps frightened, weary people recognize their longing for a place of rest and protection where they can be assured of a loving welcome.

The Homily and the Prayers

Within the structure provided by the Book of Common Prayer, people planning a funeral or memorial service can make the occasion particular to the life and death of the person who died by making specific requests for what they want to have happen at the time of the homily and the prayers. I once attended a funeral in which the name of the person who had died was never mentioned. The lessons and psalms were appropriate for the occasion, but the clergyman who conducted the service all by himself made no connection between the ritual and what the mourners were experiencing. In fact, many of us left the service feeling so dissatisfied that before we scattered we agreed to hold another funeral so that we could focus our attention on the man we had loved and on our sorrow at losing him.

The bereaved family may entrust the task of preparing a homily, or sermon, to the ordained person who will conduct the service. That can be especially valuable if the minister was well acquainted with the person who died, but it can be difficult for even an experienced preacher to sound authentic when talking about a total stranger. In either case, I think the chances of the homily being helpful to people in their grief will be increased if those who were closest to the one who died provide the minister with their recollections and insights.

An even better approach, at least in my experience, is for the bereaved people to speak for themselves. In older, simpler times people could begin working out their grief by doing what was required for the burial: washing and dressing the body, making the coffin, digging the grave. In modern society all of these tasks have been taken over by professionals, leaving the bereaved people with nothing to do unless they participate in the funeral. Only one or two can read lessons, but several can prepare and offer brief statements to take the place of the homily. Not everyone can contribute vocal or instrumental music for the service, but most people can find something to say. In one funeral the three small grandchildren of the woman who died, as well as several adults, each prepared something to say about their grandmother. At the last minute the littlest of the three handed her paper to her mother to read for her, but she will always remember that she had a part in laying her grandmother to rest.

The prayers also provide a way for people to participate and to make the ritual fit the particular occasion. Sometimes a period of silence before the spoken prayers will help people focus on their grief. Sometimes allowing people to offer individual prayers will help them to become more clear about their pain and need for healing.

At the very least, hearing the prayers from the burial service read in an unhurried fashion may lead some people to a deeper understanding of their grief. "Grant to thy faithful people pardon and peace" may suggest that part of the grief experienced by a young man was caused by the realization that he had been intending for the last several months to visit Aunt Ellen in the nursing home; now it is too late. "Give courage and faith to those who are bereaved, that they may have strength to meet the days ahead" could help a widow admit how weak and frightened she feels at the prospect of having to cope with a house, a demanding job, and two little boys all by herself. "Help us, we pray, in the midst of things we cannot understand" may permit a group of outraged neighbors realize they will never make sense out of the brutal death of a friend who had been bludgeoned by a burglar she had confronted in her living room. "Grant us grace to entrust Janet to thy never-failing love" may remind Janet's husband that taking care of her can no longer be the center of his existence and his reason for living.

The Committal

When the coffin is lowered into the grave or when the church warden covers the urn of ashes in the columbarium with a bronze plate, I am conscious that all around me the tears previously held in check have begun to flow. Sometimes the finality of the committal is the part of the ritual that most helps people to face the reality of their loss and to begin the long process of recovery. Without the sense of closure provided by interment some people cannot come to terms with their bereavement, and as a consequence, cannot begin to heal.

"Earth to earth, ashes to ashes, dust to dust." These words spoken at the committal emphasize finality. A human being is dead. A life is over. Those who remain are left in sorrow. The structure of their lives is broken. A vital piece of the whole is missing and cannot be replaced. How will they manage to put their lives back together? Death poses that question for believer and skeptic alike.

The Book of Common Prayer, from the Litany for the Dying to the Committal, points those in mourning to the way of recovery. The ancient rituals help people find a sense of community in which grieving is given a form and in which healing is made possible. By following the prompting of the rituals, even skeptics can find their way back from death to life again.

Chapter 9
SUNDAY—Other Rituals for Other Transitions

When I am on vacation or sabbatical leave, I usually go to church on Sunday morning and sit in the congregation like an ordinary layman. More often than not I leave the church feeling glad that I made the effort, but sometimes long before the service has ended, I have begun to feel bored and annoyed by the proceedings.

The mixture of reactions I experience when attending church on Sundays reminds me a little of the feelings I have developed toward swimming each weekday morning, a form of exercise to which I was condemned for life following back surgery several years ago. Many mornings when I enter the handsome building that houses our neighborhood pool, I am put off by the smell of chlorine, the murky appearance of the water, and the sight of my fellow swimmers, most of whom look much more attractive in street clothes than in bathing suits. Doing my best to ignore these negative sensations, I slip into the water and start the routine of swimming back and forth within the confines of a marked lane. After I think I have been at it for at least fifteen minutes, I check my watch and discover that no more than eight or nine minutes have passed by. I am bored, and I am angry. I am angry because the boredom reminds me of the disability that makes this boring routine necessary.

Churches often produce an atmosphere that is as offensive as that of an indoor swimming pool. The smell of a room that has been closed up all week and the sight of fussy Victorian windows and furnishings can easily offend me. The sterility of a modern building or the sound of an organ inexpertly played may produce a similar effect. I can also be put off by the tight smiles and pious expressions on the faces of the worshipers around me. Even when I do my best to ignore the negative sensations produced by the atmosphere in church, I am frequently bored almost beyond endurance. I check my watch and find the minutes dragging by. Sooner or later I am aware of my anger. I am angry because of the disability that forces me to church each week; left to my own devices, I simply do not have what it takes to live a healthy, productive life. Just as skeptics sometimes envy the inner strength they see in church people, I sometimes envy skeptics who seem to get along quite nicely without subjecting themselves to the weekly rigors of church attendance.

Although in some sense I feel compelled to swim and to attend church services, I doubt that I would continue with either discipline for very long if I could not get past the anger, the boredom, and the offensive atmosphere to find something of value. Generally I do. Sometimes in the pool I am struck by the beauty of the luminous bubbles left in the wake of the swimmer ahead of me and by the gracefulness of most human bodies when buoyed up by the water. I experience moments of delight as I realize that my body is regaining the flexibility it had lost after the previous day's exertions and the relative immobility of a night's sleep. I grow in the confidence that I will emerge feeling renewed and refreshed. In church, I gradually become aware that I can find beauty in my surroundings and that the people around me are probably quite a decent sort. We are all there for similar reasons, but reasons that are hard to explain using ordinary language in an ordinary way. We have experienced some spiritual kinks, some tightness of the soul. We anticipate the sense of renewed flexibility and refreshment that will come from the gentle exercises provided during the hour or so spent in church.

A Ritual Transition from Work Week to Work Week

One of the major gifts Christians brought to the pagan Europeans in the early centuries of the new era was the seven-day week. Unlike days, months, and years, the seven-day week did not arise from the movements of the earth and the moon, but was a human invention that Christians inherited from the Jews. Although Christians modified the pattern by setting aside the first day of the week to gather for worship instead of the last day, the rhythm remained substantially the same: six days for work and one for rest and reflection.

When skeptics become aware of the arbitrary nature of the seven-day week, they might profit from asking themselves if they are receiving the maximum benefit from this arrangement of time. It has been taken for granted over so many centuries that the original purpose can easily be forgotten. The purpose of stopping work every seventh day was not simply to take a break from the routine of labor. The seventh day was provided as an opportunity for people to put the work week and their lives in perspective. In addition, the seventh day was a time for the people to gather and to reconstitute themselves as a community. If spending Sunday morning drinking coffee and poring over the *New York Times* does not quite provide the perspective and sense of community people are looking for, they might find something of value at church.

A church service is a ritual that can provide a transition from work week to work week. Most skeptics realize that the major transitions in life, such as marriage or the birth of a child or the death of a parent, provoke feelings of anxiety and hope that must be channeled through ritual forms in order to provide useful energy. They often fail to recognize, however, that the simple transition from one week to the next provokes similar feelings that can either enhance or impair the quality of life, depending on how they are managed.

To see the value of a weekly ritual for transition, imagine the thoughts going through the mind of a supervisor in an insurance adjusting firm as he reads his newspaper and drinks his coffee on a Sunday morning. On Friday he had received another garbled, barely legible report from the claims adjuster that he had hired with some misgivings six months ago. He had hoped that the young man would develop the verbal skills he needed to do the work, but now he had to admit to himself what everyone in the office had been saying for weeks: this young man cannot do the work. The complaints about him from both the insurance companies and the people filing claims have had a demoralizing effect on all the staff. He simply must be fired. The supervisor knows what he has to do, but he takes no relish in the task. He cannot help wondering if he might have done more to help bring the young man along, or conversely, if he has caused unnecessary harm by delaying the inevitable termination of employment. The loneliest part of being a supervisor is having to tell an employee that his services are no longer desired by the company. Facing Monday morning all alone, with no way to get the emotional distance needed for the unpleasant task, the supervisor runs the risk of being unnecessarily cold or harsh with the inadequate young adjuster. Or he could be unreasonably hard on himself for having failed to see the young man's deficiencies before he hired him or for having failed to train him properly. If that supervisor had spent Sunday morning at church among people with similar concerns, if he had joined them in a ritual that allowed him to acknowledge his faults and his anxieties about dismissing an employee, he might have been equipped with a better sense of perspective with which to face the new week.

An Hour for Being Utterly Dependent

Besides being responsible for the work of a dozen claims adjusters, the supervisor also has responsibilities for his wife and their three little boys. He tries to be a good citizen by attending meetings of the civic association and the Parent-Teacher Association at the children's school. Although he normally likes his work and enjoys his family and neighborhood, sometimes all of his responsibilities weigh heavily upon him, especially on Sundays, when he has time to think about it all. As a skeptic, he had a hard time admitting how much he longed for just a few moments to get out from under all of his responsibilities and to be as utterly dependent and cared for as he had been when he was a child. Being a skeptic, he did not know that such an experience is possible each Sunday in church.

When I was in my rebellious teens, more than once I mockingly asked my mother what she got out of going to church. I knew she thought the sermons were dull and the music uninspired. Each time I asked her, she responded a little defensively, "I don't know. I just feel better all week when I've been to church on Sunday." In recent years, I think I have figured out why she felt better for the experience. When she was in church she did not have to be the caring mother and the dutiful wife and the responsible neighbor, she could just be. She did not have to do anything. Somebody else was in charge. Somebody was taking care of her. That "somebody", by the way, was not the ordained minister who was presiding. I am sure that for her, he was just the reminder that somebody else, somebody without human limitations, was looking after her.

As adults, we would be inviting trouble if we allowed ourselves, even for an hour, to regress to that infantile state where we were completely dependent on another human being. If we project our longing to be cared for onto God, however, we are relatively safe from the manipulation and antagonism that inevitably arise when we allow ourselves to become dependent on a lover, or a child, or a religious leader.

People who go to church regularly usually find that by experiencing a childlike state for an hour on Sundays, they are more likely to behave as responsible adults the rest of the week. The rhythm of movement between independence and dependence gives them the resilience they need to face the pressures of their demanding lives. A muscle that is always tense loses its strength, and a person who is always under pressure will eventually collapse. Good exercise alternates between tensing and relaxing each muscle. A good life requires a similar pattern of alternation between being independent and being dependent. Sunday morning worship can provide the moments of release we need to alternate with the six days we live in the tensions of responsibility.

The Cycle of the Church Year

Sunday morning worship, besides marking the transition from one week to the next, also emphasizes the movement from one season to another. The seasons receiving ritual emphasis in the church year have been influenced by the seasons that occur in nature, but they are not precisely the same because Christianity had already adopted annual celebrations based on Jewish agricultural festivals before the church moved into northern Europe and adapted itself to the planting and harvest cycle of a colder climate. Urban people whose lives are far removed from farms and pastures may think that they are untouched by the changing seasons, but if they allow the church to help them keep in step with the natural cycles of the year, they may find their lives enriched.

People visiting an Episcopal church from time to time throughout a year will notice the changing color scheme. The colors found on the altar and the pulpit each Sunday will be the same as the book marks in the Bible and the stoles or more elaborate vestments worn by the clergy. Each season has its distinctive color.

Each season also has a distinctive theme. These themes appear in the prayers called "collects". Each Sunday has a special collect (accent on the first syllable) in which the theme of the season and the concerns particular to the day are "collected" and offered as a prayer. The Book of Common Prayer has two complete sets of these collects, one in traditional church language beginning on page 139 and one in more contemporary English beginning on page 211.

Because the church year is a cycle and has no beginning or end, you can begin at any point, but because late summer marks the beginning of the academic year, this might be a good place to begin. The color for the season is green, a reminder of the growing season that is now drawing to an end. In northern Europe, where most of our Christian customs developed, as well as in North America, the fall is harvest time. In the early days of Christianity, and for all the centuries before, fall was not only the time when people had to gather all the food they would need to last the winter, but it was also the time to cut and stack the logs they would need for fuel and to make the repairs necessary to keep their houses snug during the cold weather. The growing and harvesting seasons coincide with the Sundays that follow the celebration of Pentecost, the last of the great spring festivals. During this period the church concentrates on the teachings of Jesus, paying special attention to the kind of behavior the followers of Jesus expect from each other.

By December the days are noticeably shorter. Primitive people may have feared that the sun was gradually losing its power and that the world would be left in cold and darkness, or wondered if they had offended the sun god, who would punish them by deserting them. Their anxiety was compounded by their memory of other winters when they ran short of food and fuel. Although high yield grains and modern systems for the storage and transportation of food, along with dependable heating systems, have largely eliminated anxiety about survival during December, people in the northern hemisphere are still affected by the diminishing light. As the darkness closes in, many people become anxious and depressed.

The church has traditionally used this time to help people focus on what they are doing with their lives and on what kind of help they need to live more fully. In church, the four Sundays preceding Christmas are known as the Sundays of Advent, and the season is identified by purple or blue.

In primitive society the period of anxiety continued until the trend toward darkness had been reversed and the sun began to rise a little earlier and set a little later each day. The recovery of the sun's strength was clearly established each year by the twenty-fifth day of December. Since before the dawn of history, people in the western Europe have set aside this day for a celebration of restored hope. They have celebrated the return of the light by creating light with bonfires and yule logs, with torches and candles, and in more recent times with electric lighting effects. They have celebrated the hope for spring and another growing season by decorating their houses with plants and trees that stay green throughout the winter. This has always been a time for eating and drinking, for exchanging greetings and gifts. Not knowing the exact date of Jesus' birth, Christians in the West adopted December 25th as his birthday while those in the East, following customs in their countries, celebrated it twelve days later, January 6th.

In Britain, Christians decided if one birthday celebration for Jesus was good, two were even better. Then, to demonstrate their devotion to festivities, if not to Jesus himself, they developed the custom of celebrating all of the days between the two as well. The first day they called Christmas, because it was the day Mass was celebrated in honor of Christ's birth; January 6th they called Epiphany, which means "light shining forth"; and all the days in between were known as the twelve days of Christmas. During the twelve days of Christmas, which Episcopal churches still observe, each church gets out its finest hangings, usually white trimmed with gold and silver.

In recent years, secular society has lost sight of the wisdom our ancestors demonstrated in attuning their lives to the natural emphasis of each season. Instead of acknowledging and making use of the anxiety that appears with the encroachment of darkness, people start decorating their houses and singing Christmas carols as soon as the Thanksgiving dishes are cleared from the table. All through December they try to ward off depression with shopping in gaily decorated malls and with office parties and social events. Then as soon as the presents are unwrapped on Christmas morning, it is all over. The gloom descends. Old quarrels are resumed with new bitterness. Individuals lose their capacity to cope. Although people are able to marshall their energy for a few hours of forced hilarity on New Year's Eve, by and large the twelve days of Christmas and the celebration of hope have disappeared from our culture. Only in those churches that possess an active memory and an appreciation for the wisdom of tradition can people today find the encouragement for facing anxiety that will prepare them for rediscovering hope.

People who appreciate the wisdom of tradition also understand the importance of celebrating hope and expressing joy. Too many of us were brought up with the notion that we do not deserve to enjoy life. We are afraid to embrace hope and give ourselves up to joy for fear that we will be caught and punished. We have inherited this unfortunate attitude from the Puritans who repudiated the Church of England and the ancient customs before establishing themselves on this side of the Atlantic. To lead healthy, balanced lives we need time to reflect on moments of gladness and to think about how we can brighten the lives of other people in the world around us. On the Sundays following the Epiphany, the church is decorated in green as a reminder that while nature sleeps under winter's blanket, energy is being stored for the new life that will emerge with spring. In the same fashion, as the worshiping community acknowledges hope and joy, the people become revitalized for the service of those who need them.

Although the hours of daylight are steadily increasing throughout January, that is often the month of the most severe cold and winter storms. By February people often wonder if spring will ever come. In primitive societies, this was the time when the food supplies began to run low, and people were often overcome with a sense of foreboding.

In Britain the final weeks of winter were called "Lent", a word derived from the same root as "lengthen", because of the lengthening days. During Lent Christians made a virtue out of necessity; the available food supply was made to last as long as possible through the practice of fasting. Christians also used this time of fasting and foreboding for self-examination. At first, only people who were preparing to join the church followed a special discipline during Lent. Later, people who had offended the community by their behavior and had been excommunicated were required to practice various forms of abstinence and prayer during this period before they could be restored to the fellowship of the church. Eventually, all Christians were urged to adopt a discipline of self-denial and an honest appraisal of their short-comings during Lent. This was a time to acknowledge the despair they felt whenever they were driven to admit how seldom they lived up to the best of which they were capable. To mark the season of Lent, the hangings in church are changed to purple fabrics or to plain burlap. On the last Sunday of Lent, when the death of Jesus is dramatized, the color may change to red.

The great spring festival in sun-worshiping societies occurred at the time of the equinox, and tribes that honored the moon-god celebrated the full moon that occurred about this time. Christians wanted to celebrate the resurrection on a Sunday at this time of year, but they also wanted to allow their converts to continue as many of their familiar practices as possible. After much controversy, Christians in western Europe settled on the first Sunday after the first full moon following the vernal equinox as the appropriate time for the celebration. English-speaking Christians did not bother to change the name of the traditional spring festival but continued to call it Easter after the pagan goddess of fertility. Christians incorporated into their celebration many of the ancient pagan symbols of fertility, such as flowers, eggs, and rabbits.

On Easter Christians bring out their hangings of white and gold, which have been stored away since Epiphany, to adorn their churches. This is the beginning of a season that emphasizes anticipation of the future. Just as in agricultural societies thoughts turn to spring planting and the hope of a bountiful fall harvest, so also in urban areas people begin to make plans for the summer and fall. This season lasts for fifty days, until the festival called Pentecost, when the hangings are changed to red to celebrate an experience of God that some said was like being touched by find and fire.

With the Sundays following Pentecost, the cycle begins anew.

A Ritual Paradigm of Human Experience

The seasons of the church year, while providing ritual support for making the most of the changing natural seasons, also offer a paradigm for understanding and appreciating all significant human experience. Read any good children's book, such as Maurice Sendak's *Where the Wild Things Are.* See an epic film like *Star Wars.* Follow the plot of one of Joseph Campbell's stories in *The Hero with a Thousand Faces.* Watch what happens to people in a therapy or training group. In nearly every case you will discover that the experience follows the pattern celebrated in the changing seasons of the church year. For example, consider the experience of the disciples of Jesus.

Curiosity: Late Pentecost. Jesus calls to some fishermen. They may know him, but they do not know him well. He intrigues them. They are curious. They want whatever he has that sets him apart from ordinary people. They follow him.

Anxiety: Advent. The disciples do not understand why Jesus will not make the most of his popularity as a healer. They do not understand most of what he tries to teach them. They are in a boat with him when a storm arises, and Jesus sleeps on a cushion in the stern. They are anxious and complain, "Teacher, do you not care if we perish?"

Hope: Christmas and Epiphany. The disciples continue to be fascinated by Jesus but they are still obviously confused. One of them, whose name is Peter, has a momentary insight. Perhaps Jesus is the messiah, the one anointed to lead Israel to freedom. Then Peter, along with James and John, has a vision of Jesus speaking with Moses and Elijah. Can it be that when they are with Jesus they are in the presence of the Lord God of Israel?

Despair: Lent. Jesus disappoints the disciples by refusing their requests for assurance and by refusing to answer their questions directly. One betrays him to the authorities. The others fall asleep when he asks them to stay with him while he prays. Peter denies ever having known him. The Roman soldiers execute Jesus. The disciples, who gave up everything to follow him, are left with nothing. They are utterly bereft and abandoned.

Anticipation: Easter to Pentecost. The disciples who did not understand Jesus, who were left with nothing at his death, find that whatever it was that made Jesus different from ordinary people is now operating in their lives. They change the course of human history.

Something like the experiences of the disciples happens to everyone. The advantage of attending church Sunday after Sunday through the cycle of a whole year is that we are reminded of the nature of all human experience. When we forget the stages that we must move through in any significant experience, such as looking for a new job or beginning a new romance, we make trouble for ourselves. If we try to wall off anxiety and despair, we also bar the possibility of real hope and anticipation. The rituals of the church year, however, remind us that we can enter into each stage of an experience in the confidence that the next stage will probably follow.

Morning and Evening Prayer

Skeptics who want to try the cycle of the church year, or who just want to sample a Sunday morning in an Episcopal church, should be prepared for either of the two possible ritual forms they may encounter: Morning Prayer or the Holy Eucharist.

Some Episcopal churches have Morning Prayer every Sunday except the first Sunday of the month and festival days like Easter and Pentecost. Because Morning Prayer has very little ritual action, skeptics sometimes have trouble relating to the service. They often make the mistake of concentrating on the words, or they simply become bored and tune out. To get anything out of Morning Prayer, a person has to understand the origins and purpose of this form of worship.

In ancient Israel the day began and ended with sacrifices in the temple at Jerusalem. Devout Jews who did not have ready access to the temple frequently gathered in synagogues each morning and evening for prayers, the recitation of psalms, and the reading of Scripture. Christians often followed this practice, especially after Christianity was recognized as a legitimate religion by the emperor Constantine in the fourth century. Often the monks and nuns gathered more frequently for devotions, as many as seven times each day, but the ordinary Christians met with them just at the beginning and the ending of the working day.

The Daily Morning and Evening Prayer services in the prayer book evolved from these ancient Jewish and Christian customs. Originally they were not simply Sunday rituals, but a daily practice. One value of reading or singing the daily offices (as they are sometimes called) on Sundays in church is that the services provide a reminder of the passage people must navigate each morning as their place on the earth moves out of the shadows into the light of the sun and each evening as they face the coming darkness.

Morning Prayer on Sundays can celebrate the daily transition from the nameless terrors of the dark to the promise of new possibilities that appear with the dawn. Children often seem to have an inborn fear of the dark. Military veterans who were traumatized by combat often relive the horrors of their experience when they lie in bed at night. Middle-aged people sometimes wake up staring into the darkness with the realization that someday they will surely die. The first rays of the sun usually bring reassurance. Courage returns. Another day begins. Many people over the ages have discovered that they begin the day with more energy and enthusiasm if they mark the transition from darkness to light with an appropriate ritual.

A daily ritual can also facilitate the transition from being asleep in bed to being alert at work. Alternating activity and rest in a regular cycle every twenty-four hours is essential for mental and physical health. Many people find getting started in the morning to be a difficult task. Facing a new day means not just the promise of new possibilities but the burden of old responsibilities and the threat of unanticipated problems. The daily transition from rest to work carries some of the same emotional freight observed at the major life passages. Joining a congregation in Morning Prayer even once a week on Sundays can help a person keep alert to the kind of routine that may be necessary to facilitate the transition from rest to work each day.

Some churches also offer Evening Prayer each Sunday. The form, the origins, and the purpose of Evening Prayer are similar to those of Morning Prayer, but customarily more of the evening prayer service is set to music, hence its popular name, "Evensong". Although Sunday Evensong is more popular in England than in the United States, a skeptic determined to try out this form of worship can probably find the service offered in some church in nearly every large, metropolitan area.

How to Appreciate Morning or Evening Prayer

A skeptic who has experimented with some form of meditation or taken some training in stress reduction will have an easier time appreciating the value of Morning or Evening Prayer than someone with no experience in what is often called "centering". Anyone willing to practice, however, can learn to suspend logic and let the rhythm of the language and the imagery of the words calm an overly active mind, relax a tense body, and soothe a troubled spirit.

The most important thing to remember when beginning one of the daily offices is that these services originated in the East and were popularized in the West by people following a monastic discipline. These people were not trying to analyze the words they used, nor were they trying to understand religion. Instead, they were attempting to open themselves to the mystery of God's presence. When the forms now used for Morning and Evening Prayer were developed in ancient Judaism and early Christianity, logical analysis had not yet been deified and the scientific method had not yet been invented. When people gathered to recite the psalms, to read Scripture, and to pray, they were attempting to move beyond the limits of logic and to experience truth inwardly. To appreciate one of the daily offices in a contemporary setting, a person must be willing to recognize that in a search for truth logic can do only so much and no more. Logic can bring us close to the mystery of human existence, but to enter the mystery we must leave logic behind.

Morning and Evening Prayer frequently begin with a confession of sin. That is an opportunity to let go of the past, to put aside failure as well as guilt. Confession also offers a way of getting out of normal habits of thinking and a way of becoming open to new ideas.

Much of the time spent at the daily offices is devoted to the reading or singing of psalms and other ancient poems, known as canticles, which are taken from the literature that was sacred to the early Christians. Over the ages people have discovered that saying or chanting these poems on a regular basis makes them feel more integrated, less fragmented. If you find yourself in a church where people are chanting the psalms and canticles, and the music is not familiar to you, you can just listen and let the sound engulf you and carry you along. As you gradually become accustomed to the repeated patterns of the music, you can join in and let the sound of your own voice contribute to the experience.

Between the canticles, people participating in Morning or Evening Prayer sit quietly to hear passages read from the Bible. In this setting, they make a mistake if they try to interpret what they hear or even understand the meaning of the words. They would find greater profit from the service if they could just let the images conveyed by the words enter their awareness and condition their attitudes on a subconscious level.

A similar attitude can enhance an appreciation for the prayers that conclude the service. Skeptics will not get much out of the service if they are fretting over all of the reasons why praying is an absurd practice. All of the obstacles noted in the chapter on personal prayer can certainly get in the way of corporate prayer. The way around the barriers in corporate prayer is to assume that the words of the prayers have been designed to help the worshipers identify concerns that may have been lurking just below the surface. Once they have identified their real concerns, they are more likely to take constructive action. In congregations that permit individuals to pray aloud during this part of the service, the prayers also serve as announcements of particular joys and sorrows. Information received in this context may also stimulate some people to respond, such as by writing a note of congratulation to the couple who has a new baby, or by offering to take care of two small children for an evening so that their father can visit their mother who is in the hospital. Sometimes the information simply helps the members of the congregation to appreciate the diversity of their concerns. They may have a better under- standing of their community when they learn that one person is on his way to a world hunger conference in Africa, while another has a colleague who is suffering the first symptoms of AIDS.

Frequently Morning or Evening Prayer on Sundays will in- clude hymns, an offering, and a sermon. Episcopalians are not noted for their hymn singing, and sermons vary enormous- ly in quality, so the skeptical visitor should not expect too much from these added elements, but the offering provides a consis- tent spiritual possibility: the opportunity to experience your- self as a generous and expansive person. You can, of course, get something out of hymns even when they are badly sung by finding poetic images to occupy your mind for a moment. You can even get something of value from a poor sermon. You can hear the preacher make what for you is an absurd statement, and then you can stop listening and carry on an in- ternal argument about the point. When the argument in your head has spent itself, you can tune into the sermon again long enough to find something else which offends you and repeat the process. If you follow this advice, you will not leave the service with a feeling that you have wasted your time.

The Holy Eucharist

The alternative to Morning or Evening Prayer for Sunday worship in the Episcopal Church has been known by a variety of names—Holy Communion, the Lord's Supper, the Divine Liturgy, the Mass, the Holy Mysteries—but now it is most com- monly called the Holy Eucharist. Each of the names em- phasizes some particular aspect of the ancient ritual meal. "Communion" points to the sharing of bread and wine as well as the partnership established among the people and with God. "The Lord's Supper" recalls that the practice began with the last supper Jesus ate with his disciples. The word "litur- gy" comes from the Greek word meaning "work", suggesting that the performance of the ritual is one of the primary tasks undertaken by the followers of Jesus. "Mass" evolved from the last words of the service in Latin addressed to the congregation by the celebrant: *Ite, missa est,* "Go, you are dismissed," a reminder that the service is intended to prepare people for going back into the world. The word "mysteries" hints at participation in the impenetrable secrets of the universe. "Eucharist", derived from the Greek words "good + favor", came to indicate the response people make when they feel that they have received beneficial gifts from God. Eucharist is a ritual which provides people with a form for expressing gratitude or thanks for all of the good things of life.

Even taken all together, the names for the ritual meal do not define its real meaning for the skeptical visitor to an Episcopal church. The skeptic will find meaning primarily through participating in the ritual action and by allowing the images and symbols of the rite to stimulate new ways of understanding. With this approach, the skeptic may find that the Eucharist can provide a ritual for a variety of common transitions.

A Ritual for Transition

At the beginning of the Eucharist, visitors who have sampled Morning or Evening Prayer may not see much difference in the proceedings. The Eucharist often opens with singing and always includes readings from the Bible and prayers. It usually includes a selection from the psalms and a confession. Skeptics who have difficulty with the language in this part of the service can participate on the same basis as they might have in the daily offices. After the sermon and offering, however, the Eucharist offers ritual possibilities not available in the other rites of the church.

The action begins with representatives of the congregation bringing bread and wine, along with the money given by the people, to the altar or communion table. These things represent reality on at least three levels. First, the reality of our dependence on nature to provide us with food and drink: the grain that was ground into flour and the grapes that were crushed to make wine came from the earth. Second, the reality of our dependence on other people for survival— farmers, millers, and bakers; the laborers who pick the grapes and the technicians who oversee the fermentation of the wine; the truck drivers, wholesalers, grocers, and all the others who make food and drink available. Third, the reality of our dependence on a source of strength and joy and triumph that remains as mysterious to us as did the working of yeast in the dough and in the wine vat to people of earlier times.

The celebrant pours out the wine into a cup and breaks the bread. The symbols of our unity in mutual dependence are divided. The broken bread and the wine poured out often remind me of broken promises and spilled tears, of shattered dreams and bitter disappointments, of being separated from people I love, and of feeling torn apart inside.

The ritual action of Communion reminds me of a painful telephone conversation a couple in our congregation once had with one of their grown daughters. Their daughter, who had graduated from college two years earlier, was living in a distant city and doing well in her chosen field. In the middle of telling them about her thoughts of traveling to Africa or South America before starting graduate school, she stopped to complain, "You never tell me what you think about my plans. No matter what I say, you don't react." Her parents protested that she was a grown woman and perfectly capable of making her own decisions, and that they had no desire to interfere in her life. In truth, they quite prided themselves in being the kind of parents who encourage their children to live their own lives. Their daughter's complaint, however, was that in not reacting one way or another to her announced plans, they were treating her as if she did not have suffiecient confidence in herself to make up her own mind after receiving their advice. At the same time, they were depriving her of the wisdom they had gained by experience. Her accusations hurt them because she spoke a truth that they had failed to see. In withholding their opinions, they had not been treating her with the respect they owed to a responsible and capable adult whom they loved. In that moment, they felt like failures as parents. The bonds that they thought had held their family together had been broken by their insensitivity.

As they continued to talk, however, they realized that their daughter had forgiven their misguided behavior even before she had lodged her complaint. In fact, if she did not love them, she would not have opened up a conversation that she knew would be painful for all of them. Before they hung up the telephones that day, the three of them felt closer than ever.

That is the way life is. To find our unity we must first be broken. In reflecting on that momentary rupture in family relationships, I can see what happened to that family dramatized in the ritual of individuals gathering to eat the broken bread and to drink the poured-out wine. As we share the bread and the wine we acknowledge both what is broken and what has been restored. When healing has already taken place, the ritual drama provides an occasion for gratitude and celebration. In this fashion the Eucharist becomes a ritual for transition from weakness to strength, from sorrow to joy, from tragedy to triumph. During nearly every week most of us have an experience worth marking with such a ritual. We may not talk about such mundane transitions with other people, but we can find by inwardly marking such events at the Sunday Eucharist that our lives gain intensity and that we acquire wisdom.

When I participate in communion during a crisis, and my connections with other people are still broken, the ritual shows me the way to confidence and hope. Our unity may be restored when together we can acknowledge what has become fragmented. Many people in our society try to maintain peace in the family or in the office by refusing to acknowledge the divisions that everyone knows exist. Denial may work for a time, but never for very long. The first sign that denial is not working is when people complain of boredom. The second sign is a loss of energy. The third sign is an eruption of anger and acrimony. People who participate regularly in the Eucharist receive a valuable reminder of the steps they will have to take. They will have to pass through a time of weakness, sorrow, and even tragedy if they are going to find their way to strength, joy, and triumph.

The Last Supper

Before distributing the bread and wine, the celebrant always tells the story of Jesus' last supper with his disciples. If skeptics have been able to identify with the experience of the disciples as described in the gospels, they will probably be able to see something of their lives reflected in what happened to the followers of Jesus on the night before he died.

Jesus had done his best to let his friends in on the secret of his confidence and authority, but he had failed miserably in the attempt. His disciples wanted to be dependent on him. They wanted him to make their lives work for them. They wanted to draw their strength from his faith. Apparently Jesus realized that these people would never discover for themselves the qualities that had attracted them to him as long as he was with them. When he sensed that the Roman occupation authorities, who feared he was trying to lead a revolt, would probably arrest and execute him, he made one last attempt to help his disciples discover what he had been trying to convey to them. He joined them for one last meal at the time of the Passover. During the course of the meal, when he blessed the bread and wine, he told them that in the future they were to eat and drink in remembrance of him.

Fortunately for future generations, after the death of Jesus at least some of those who had been present at that last supper remembered his words. They ate bread and drank wine in his memory. In so doing, they saw at last what they had failed to hear during his life.

Jesus could not give these people authority and confidence. The only way he could reach them was to become as weak and helpless as they were. In his weakness and helplessness he entered their lives. He became one of them. When his followers realized what he had done, they were overwhelmed by the feeling that when they had been with him they had been in the presence of the Lord God of Israel. Now that Jesus was gone, they sensed within themselves the authority and confidence that they had admired in him. It was as if his essence, or spirit, had become part of their lives as individuals and as a community. In that spirit they discovered their mission was to bring their discovery to the rest of the human race. To do so, however, they would have to do as Jesus did. In their new-found strength, they would have to experience weakness and helplessness to make the Lord God of Israel known.

Skeptics do not have to believe that the Lord God of Israel exists or that the last supper was a historical event in order to see the truth to which the ritual meal is pointing. People help other people when they find common ground. If a colleague at work loses his wife, you cannot console him by telling him about your great marriage. You may feel uncomfortable because of his obvious grief, but if you attempt to cheer him up so that you can be relieved of your discomfort, you are not likely to provide him with any genuine insight or comfort. In fact, you are more apt to push him toward depression. What makes you feel embarrassed is the realization that you can do nothing to fix the situation. If you are willing to experience your helplessness and weakness in the face of your colleague's grief, however, you may be able to be with him in a way that will enhance both of your lives.

The life of each Christian community revolves around the gatherings on Sundays. Each Sunday the community provides a ritual that assists the people who gather in making the transition from experience to experience, from one day to the next, from work week to work week, and from season to season. Christians over the ages have found that the Sunday rituals enable them to negotiate these transitions with more awareness and grace than they would find if left to their own devices. Skeptics may make the same discovery, but they need to be warned that the Sunday rituals may not seem like much help on first or second try. It may take a while for the Sunday routine to become a part of the life-giving pattern of Christian life.

Appendix

***

Case Study:
Finding An
Episcopal
Church

Looking for a suitable Episcopal church in an urban area can be a daunting task for even the most determined skeptic. For example, people living in the nation's capital who are willing to spend up to forty-five minutes getting to an Episcopal church, can choose from nearly one hundred congregations. The task is much simpler in small towns and rural areas where Episcopal churches are few and far between. For that reason, the advice in the first part of this chapter is aimed primarily at skeptics living in major metropolitan areas where a bewildering variety of Episcopal churches is available, but the observations may be useful in helping the rural or small town skeptic in deciding if the Episcopal church is a real option. The suggestions in the rest of the chapter, from getting started onward, should apply to any location.

What to Look For

Churches, like people, develop definite personalities. Every congregation is different from every other congregation, and even a small congregation is a complex organism that cannot be understood and evaluated at a glance. Like individual people, congregations reveal their natures through a variety of clues provided by reputation, appearance, and behavior.

Reputation

The vast majority of people locate churches through the recommendations of their friends and acquaintances. In looking for an Episcopal church, you can start with your neighbors and office mates, casually asking if they have heard of an Episcopal church in the area that is not too particular about what their members believe. People who rarely go to church as well as people who go to churches of other denominations often have information about Episcopal parishes, or they have become aware of churches that are particularly active in their neighborhoods. Following this approach, in a relatively short time an interested person can often develop a list of the local Episcopal churches whose reputations are promising.

If an informal canvassing of personal contacts does not produce any useful leads, all is not lost. Other methods for checking on the reputations of churches can be equally valuable. The simplest is to look in the Yellow Pages and call Episcopal churches at random. Ask the parish secretaries, or the clergy, or the volunteers who answer the telephone if they know of any church in the area with a reputation for being open-minded. If they claim that reputation for themselves, they are certainly worth investigating. If they concede that reputation to another church, they probably do so on the basis of sound information.

Another way to check on the reputation of an Episcopal church is to call the bishop's secretary. The people who work most closely with the bishops in the Episcopal Church know everything that is going on and know every church at least by reputation. Sometimes their information is skewed, but generally speaking, they know what the individual churches are like. If they do not, they will refer callers to other people on the bishop's staff who carry titles like archdeacon, or canon to the ordinary, or executive officer. Such staff people often work directly with the congregations and can provide first-hand information about what each is really like. To find the bishop's office, look in the telephone directory under "Diocese of . ." or "Episcopal Diocese of . ." or "Episcopal Church House" to see if a bishop resides in your city. If you cannot find a bishop that way, just call any Episcopal church and ask for the telephone number of the diocesan office.

Appearance

Winston Churchill observed that people shape their buildings and then the buildings shape the people. A visitor can pick up a sense of a congregation's history and values from the buildings in which they meet and worship. Some skeptics are drawn to architecture that reflects a strong appreciation of the ancient traditions through the use of Gothic, Norman, or Romanesque forms. Others are taken by the simplicity of modern structures that suggests a sensitivity to contemporary life. Some are attracted by an awareness of mystery represented by a high altar far removed from the people and the stress of their everyday lives, while others appreciate the sense of community suggested by a central table around which the people gather to share in the symbolic meal. Stained glass windows are an art form that opens up new dimensions of reality for some people, but a glimpse of sky and trees is more helpful to others seeking an awareness of God's presence. When skeptics find a church where the architecture is congenial to their point of view, they have a good possibility of discovering congenial people.

Buildings also yield clues about the congregation through the ways in which they are used. Are the buildings clean enough to suggest people with self-respect, or are they depressingly tidy, suggesting that no real life is permitted? Are there signs that the buildings are available during the week for use by community groups, or does the congregation jealously guard its sacred space? Has appropriate space been provided for the children, or do their needs appear to dominate the concerns of the parish? Visitors can find answers to these and other questions just by wandering about the buildings in odd hours. If the buildings are locked, a sign will usually indicate the hours the church office is open and when someone will be available to unlock the doors.

While wandering about the building, the visitor can pick up other clues about the congregation. Bulletin boards, banners, and literature for sale or for the taking all indicate the interests of some members of the congregation or of the clergy.

Seeing the building during a quiet period may be quite different from seeing the same place when the congregation has gathered for worship. Sometimes the appearance of the people overshadows the appearance of the buildings, but what the people look like also provides the visitor with important information. Because religion is both a personal and a tribal affair, people find as a rule that worship is most satisfactory when they are worshiping with people much like themselves. Skeptics sometimes have a hard time accepting their natural instinct to be with people like themselves, thinking that they should want to spend more time with poor people or people of different racial backgrounds, but parish life works best when parishioners have common attitudes and interests. Churches with a racial and cultural mix exist, but by examining them closely the visitor will likely find them to be congregations in transition from one kind of people to another. Most skeptics would be better off in a more stable community with a clear sense of its own identity.

A look around the congregation will show the visitor something about the age range, the income levels, and the culture from which the members have been drawn to a particular church. At this time the most important question for the visitor will be, "Are these my kind of folks?" Unless skeptics feel that they are among kindred spirits, they are not likely to feel that they can press their questions and admit the reservations they have about Christianity. Unless they can be honest about their skepticism, they will not be able to find much of value in being associated with a church.

Behavior

The Sunday morning visitor may have a difficult time trying to evaluate the behavior of a congregation. Some of the behavioral clues as to the true nature of the membership are quite subtle. Take the question of friendliness, for example. Most Episcopalians are fairly reserved by nature, causing some visitors to assume that they are not welcome. An open display of friendliness to strangers, however, might not be so much an indication of warmth and acceptance as it would be a sign of desperation from a group trying to recruit new members in order to survive.

In observing the behavior of the people in an unfamiliar church, the skeptic would do better to pay attention to the way they behave with each other than the way they treat visitors. If the skeptic decides to affiliate, the way visitors are treated will soon become irrelevant, but the standards for interaction among members will have a profound impact on the church experience. As the skeptic observes the members of the church, certain questions are important: How respectful are adults to each other? How do they treat the children? To what extent are people able to demonstrate their feelings? Are they able to laugh and cry, to show affection and anger? How open do they appear to be about their differences of opinion? What are the signs that they care about each other? What concerns seem uppermost on the minds of the members? How enthusiastic do people seem to be about their church?

One Sunday morning after the service, a visitor complimented me on the relaxed formality of the worship and then went on to say that she did not think that this was the church for her. She had observed the intensity of the interactions among the members and their enthusiasm for what they were doing. "If I started coming to your church, I just know I would get drawn in and want to be involved in everything. I don't have time for that kind of involvement at this stage of my life. I want to find a church where I can slip in quietly from time to time without being noticed and without feeling left out." By observing the congregation on just one visit, she was able to see that we were not the kind of church she wanted.

Granted that the observations of a visitor will produce data of limited quality, the clues are still important. In fact, sometimes these first impressions are more objective than later ones.

What to Look Out For

Not all Episcopal churches will do for skeptical people. Many of the churches that might not do for skeptics, however, make their position known through code words. Some of the words should be taken as a definite stop sign and others simply suggest that caution is in order. The code words will appear on sign boards outside the church, in advertising, and on the literature produced by the congregation.

Stop Signs

Charismatic: Episcopalians often describe themselves as charismatics if they are given to ecstatic utterances—called "speaking in tongues"—and extreme exuberance in their worship. They tend to raise their arms when they sing and pray. The reason such churches will not do for skeptics is that charismatics generally treat the Bible as if it were dictated by God. In other words, they are "true believers" according to the definition I use: people who hold to a body of opinion or a system of propositions in the face of contrary evidence; people who think that all who hold opposing opinions are in error and morally inferior.

Renewal: Renewal is a code word charismatic Episcopalians use to identify their churches. Others in the Episcopal Church also use the word to describe congregations that once were dull and boring but have found new life. Most of those who use the term, however, are true believers of one sort or another. They talk about being renewed by the Holy Spirit and sprinkle their conversations liberally with words like "spiritual" and "fellowship", but unless they see an opportunity for a conversion, they rarely show much affection for people who do not share their beliefs.

1928 Book of Common Prayer: The Episcopal Church in the United States adopted a revised prayer book in 1979. The first prayer book in English appeared in 1549 and has been revised periodically ever since, both in England and in the various Anglican national church bodies throughout the world. Congregations that have refused to use the new prayer book are for the most part made up of true believers. One of their beliefs is that the only language adequate for worship is the kind of English spoken in the days of King James I. Although the 1979 Book of Common Prayer provides for some rituals using the antique language, some Episcopalians resent the presence of the modern language forms and are upset by other changes. Many of these people who idolize the 1928 book also object to the ordination of women, and were angered by the gender-inclusive language employed in the 1982 Hymnal approved for use in Episcopal churches.

Code Words Requiring Caution

Evangelical: Some Episcopalians who call themselves evangelical are actually charismatics. Others who use the word to describe themselves hold many views that are indistinguishable from those of the charismatics, but they are not given to ecstatic utterances and they do not necessarily hold up their arms when they sing and pray. Not all evangelicals, however, are true believers. Some use the word in the original sense of "those who spread the good news." They may be quite open to the needs and concerns of skeptical people because they have a tradition of respect for the opinions of the laity.

Catholic: Some Episcopal churches use the term "catholic" to indicate that they are committed to worship in a medieval style and to providing a ministry to the poor, the sick, and the hungry. They usually call Holy Communion the "mass", and they refer to their priest as "Father". Some Episcopalians who cherish the catholic tradition have a high regard for intellectual integrity, but this is not true for all of them. Many Anglo-Catholics, as they often call themselves, emphasize the authority of the clergy at the expense of the laity and place great confidence in the efficacy of their esoteric rites and rituals. In short, Anglo-Catholics *may* be true believers with a low level of tolerance for the presence of skeptics in their midst.

Anglican: Technically this adjective identifies all of the churches that trace their roots to the Church of England.

Unfortunately, many congregations that emphasize the term in advertising their presence do so to differentiate themselves from other Episcopalians. They claim that they are maintaining the true Anglican tradition while others have strayed from the path by doing such things as revising the prayer book and ordaining women. Such an attitude is typical of true believers and should be a warning to skeptics that they would have to change their convictions in order to be welcome among the "Anglicans".

How to Get Started

Once skeptical people have discovered a promising Episcopal church, they must spend some time at the next level of investigation to see if this particular church is going to work for them. They can shorten the time required, however, if they will take advantage of the opportunities for serious inquiry available to visitors in most Episcopal churches.

Coffee Hour

Coffee hour at a typical Episcopal church provides an opportunity for you to discover what the congregation is really like, but to take advantage of the opportunity you must be both bold and determined. When the worship service ends and the people gather at one end of the church or adjourn to an adjacent hall, the visitor is often overwhelmed by a sea of backs. It is often amazing how few faces appear among the backs at a coffee hour, and those that do appear are quickly turned away. You quickly get the impression that everyone else in the room is engaged in earnest conversation. That impression produces a feeling of rejection and of profound isolation prompting, all but the most bold and determined to escape quickly.

Under such conditions, you will do well to recall that Episcopalians tend to be rather reserved and are not likely to introduce themselves to a visitor for fear the person may be a long-time member whose face they have forgotten. That fear is compounded after your third or fourth Sunday morning appearance because by then your face will be familiar—causing the members to think they have simply forgotten your name. As long as you understand that the people at the coffee hour are not trying to be exclusive, you may be able to keep most rejection anxieties under control long enough to start a conversation.

Understanding other dynamics of the coffee hour may also increase your courage. If you are aware of feeling excluded because of all the animated conversations going on around the room, you can also recognize that all of those other people who belong to the church feel included because they have something to say to each other. They are eager to see each other and to catch up on the week's events. They have church business to transact and social engagements to plan. These people are busy with each other because they are a community that gathers as a whole only once a week, and they need the time to connect with one another. If all they did at coffee hour was to look for visitors, they would not be a community but a religious sales force. So you can take heart by remembering that all of these people were once excluded visitors. Over the course of time each one of them had become included in the life of the community.

Normally, the visitor must make the first move to get acquainted. This can be done by anyone willing to call upon all available reservoirs of social strength, to walk straight up to a stranger, to take a deep breath, and to make an introduction followed by, "I'm new here. How long have you been coming to this church?" If you discover the other person is a visitor also, no harm is done. The two of you can compare notes before separating to continue your investigations.

If you do not want to waste time by talking with other visitors, this situation can easily be avoided. A moment's observation will quickly reveal the other visitors. They will be studying the details of the stained glass windows as if they were entranced by them. Or they will be lingering at the coffee pot, taking an inordinately long time in filling their cups and stirring in the sugar and cream. Or they will be standing up against the wall with a fixed gaze at an invisible object just above the heads of everyone in the room. Often their discomfort sends out vibrations that only the most insensitive person can miss. If you want to talk with a church member, you must look for someone who appears to be at home in the coffee hour.

Once you find a genuine member, any question about the church or the member's participation in the life of the congregation is fair to ask. For example: "What attracted you to this church?""How are you involved, besides coming on Sunday mornings?""What are the clergy like?""What do you think of the sermons?""What programs or activities are open to people like me?""What is the best way to get started if I decide to join?"

Official People

As the visitor's questions become more particular and technical, the member may well introduce the visitor to some official person. The official person may be someone designated as an usher or greeter, or it may be the man or woman seated near a "Welcome Table" sign.

In some congregations the official people most likely to welcome visitors are the elected representatives of the congregation. The two lay officials with the most authority are called "wardens". The other elected leaders are known as members of the "vestry", a church board of directors on which the wardens also sit. These are both antique terms, but their meanings are not difficult to discern. A warden is a "keeper"; one warden usually takes care of the church finances and organization while the other takes care of the building and grounds. A vestry is a body that the community has "vested" with the authority to carry on the business of the church. Vesting originally meant "clothing", a reference to the robes of office, but vestries today receive authority without distinctive garments.

Appointed and elected officials are usually an excellent source of information, but the visitor should not rely upon them to the exclusion of continued conversations with ordinary members.

Meeting the Clergy

Visitors with probing questions may quickly find themselves being introduced to one of the clergy. People with no background in the Episcopal Church sometimes are confused about titles and proper forms of address when being introduced to the ordained ministers. The following definitions will help prepare the visitor for an encounter with Episcopal clergy.

First, the titles:

A *rector* is a priest who has been elected by the vestry to preside at the worship services and meetings of the congregation, to ensure an adequate program of education and music, and to provide services to the members in times of tragedy or transition. "Rector" comes from the Latin word meaning "ruler", but rectors in the Episcopal church are not permitted to rule. They share authority with their vestries.

A *vicar* is a priest who has been appointed, usually by the bishop, to do all the things a rector does. "Vicar" comes from the same Latin root as "vicarious" and identifies one who acts on behalf of another.

A *curate* is a priest (or a *deacon*, if the curate happens to be serving an internship in the first year after graduating from theological school) who assists the senior priest. Originally a curate was one who was given responsibility for a "cure of souls", meaning the care of Christians.

An *associate rector* is a priest who has been given a modern title to grant more dignity than "curate" conveys, often in recognition for increased responsibility.

A *permanent deacon* is an ordained person who does not aspire to the priesthood. People who bear this title usually earn their livings outside of the church and serve the church in the evenings and on weekends. In biblical times the deacons were charged with the care of widows and orphans. Interest in reviving this function has recently surfaced, but most deacons today exercise their office primarily at worship services.

A *bishop* is a priest who has been elected by the clergy and representatives of the congregations to oversee the work of the church in their geographical area, called a diocese. "Bishop" comes from a Greek word that meant literally an "overseer".

A *dean* is the senior priest on the staff of a cathedral. A cathedral can be any church where the bishop's chair, or *cathedra*, resides. Since the bishop is frequently away visiting parishes in the diocese, the dean often functions much like a rector in a parish church. "Dean" has evolved into English from the Latin *decanus*, a title that originally meant the chief of ten men.

A *canon* is a priest who is an assistant to the bishop or to the dean of a cathedral, or who has been given an honorary title for services rendered the bishop. "Canon" is a Greek word meaning "rod" or "rule".

Then, the forms of written address:

For most of the Episcopal clergy, the appropriate honorific is "The Reverend" (or The Rev.) preceding the formal name. The honorific, of course, is never used with a nickname or with the surname alone. Bishops are addressed "The Rt. Rev.", deans "The Very Rev.", and canons "The Rev. Canon".

Finally, the rules for addressing Episcopal clergy in face to face conversation, important only if you want to evoke a warm and sympathetic response: 1. Never under any circumstances use the honorific, either by itself or with a name in speaking directly to an ordained minister in the Episcopal Church. Never say something like, "Good morning, Reverend" or "Hello, Reverend Adams." 2. Do not address clergy by their titles if they are rectors, curates, or associates. For instance, you would not say, "I am pleased to have met you, Rector" or "I am planning to take your seminar, Curate Jones." 3. You may use the title with or without the surname in speaking to bishops, deans, and canons. With vicars, you may use the title only by itself, without the name appended. For example, you could say, "Thank you, Bishop" or "Thank you, Bishop Walker." You would ask, "May I have a word with you, Vicar?" but never "Vicar Williams." 4. If you want to be formal, but have not yet picked any clues from the congregation, you may always ask the clergy directly how they prefer to be addressed. Some are accustomed to "Father" or "Mother". Others prefer Mr. or Ms., and this usage is usually safe. 5. Many Episcopal churches are quite informal and the clergy prefer to be called by their Christian names. If so, they will let you know.

This may seem unnecessarily complicated, but the great array of antique titles and forms of address are part of the paraphernalia that goes with an ancient tradition. Once the visitor has figured out what to call the clergy, however, the next step at becoming introduced to the church is easy: call the church office and make an appointment with one of the ordained ministers. As a rule the clergy are not especially helpful on Sunday mornings. They are distracted by responsibilities for organizing the worship and for keeping a sermon in mind. Many of them can remember little of what they are told just before or after a service. Your introductory conversation with one of the clergy will be much more productive on any day other than Sunday. Also, in a private conversation with a skeptic, the clergy can be much more informative and responsive than is possible when they are surrounded by members and other visitors wanting attention.

Often the clergy, besides responding to the skeptical person's immediate concerns, will recommend particular ways of getting started in the church. Some parishes have meetings or suppers for newcomers so that they can get to know each other, meet some of the church leaders, and find out more about the church. Some may have groups or classes for new people that meet for a limited number of sessions. Attending either these one-evening gatherings or the short-term classes can save the inquiring skeptic time in the long run. Such experiences will demonstrate quickly if the particular church will provide an appropriate arena for the exploration of serious, unanswerable questions.

Joining and Belonging

What the skeptical person needs to do in order to affiliate with an Episcopal church depends upon the person's previous Christian experience. A person who has been baptized in any denomination can be enrolled as a member in most Episcopal churches simply by making a pledge of financial support. A person who has never been baptized must usually take instruction, either privately or in a group, before being admitted as a member through the ritual of baptism.

Church members, that is, baptized people who support the church financially, are known as "communicants" if they receive communion regularly. As a rule, communicants can vote and hold office in the church, but another level of membership is also open to them. Adult communicants can become "confirmed communicants" if they want to make a public profession of faith in the presence of a bishop. Most skeptics would probably not want to take the latter step without giving the matter serious consideration. This book was written to show how skeptics can in good conscience become confirmed communicants of the Episcopal Church, but just reading it would not be adequate preparation. You would also want to participate in what is usually called an adult confirmation class or an inquirers' class before deciding if a public profession of faith is appropriate.

Episcopal churches vary in the amount of stress they place on the two different levels of membership. Some pay little attention to the difference between communicant members and confirmed communicants, while others see the distinction as representing the practical difference between joining a community and belonging to it. What you join, you can quit. When you belong, you recognize within yourself a commitment to the ideals of the organization and a responsibility for the life of the community; you cannot simply walk away if you become angry or disenchanted. Joining is putting your name on a list and paying your dues. Belonging is becoming a member of the family. Most of the value in being associated with an Episcopal church comes from belonging, even if the congregation does not identify that status by its formal name, confirmed communicant.

How to Get What You Want from Church

You may not always be able to get what you want from an Episcopal church, but you can improve your chances by learning something about internal parish politics and about the care and feeding of the church staff.

For some skeptics "politics" is a dirty word. Although I admit that I am sometimes tempted to use the word in a pejorative sense, I usually catch myself by remembering a lesson I learned from my father. He had found wisdom in the old saying about politics, "That is the price we must pay for the privilege of governing ourselves." Episcopal parishes are self- governing organizations and, as such, cannot function without politics.

The political life of a parish includes the election of the wardens and other members of the vestry. In an Episcopal church, the vestry has the authority to make most of the major decisions: engaging the services of clergy, raising and spending money, buying and selling property, erecting and maintaining buildings. This is a "republican" form of government rather than the pure democracy of a town meeting, but that does not mean that all power resides in the vestry. Other sources of power are often available to anyone who is interested. You may decide to aim for a seat on the vestry, but before such a try would be likely to succeed, you must have demonstrated a capacity to assume and to use authority responsibly in some other area of parish life.

The quickest way to acquire power in a church is to find a job that everybody agrees is important but that nobody wants to do. For example, in the parish I serve, an outspoken skeptic discovered that no one was willing to edit the parish newsletter. He volunteered, added new features, improved the quality of writing, and enlisted the support of additional volunteers to get the monthly publication printed and mailed. Within two years he was firmly established as a leader in the congregation and ran successfully for a contested seat on the vestry. Such a rapid rise is not unusual. People who are willing to work generally acquire influence rapidly.

Before running for office in an Episcopal church, however, skeptics might do well do remind themselves what they were looking for in their affiliation with a religious community. The first chapter of this book lists seven areas in which skeptical people might find something of value in the church: community, ritual, ethics, meaning, identity, reassurance, and a longing for God. Formal parish politics might help the skeptic find a sense of community and identity, but getting something in all seven areas will most often require work in the arena of informal politics.

Informal Political Maneuvering

Suppose that the skeptic, while still struggling with much of the language in the Sunday morning worship, nevertheless has come to value the ritual. And suppose also that the skeptic finds that the music is frequently disappointing. New members, including skeptics, often assume that their only options are to complain or to look for another church. The person who understands how parishes work will take another approach: find a way of doing something about the situation. That way will be to work into a position of influence where constructive suggestions will be assured of a hearing. If you can sing, volunteering for the choir is a good place to begin, and offering to help with the organizational life of the choir is a good second step. If you have no ability in making music, however, all is not lost. Many parishes have something known as a worship committee or a liturgy committee. Some even have a committee devoted exclusively to music. If such committees exist, people can usually get on them simply by volunteering. Some may require evidence of prior commitment, such as a willingness to usher or to help set up the church for worship services, but in no case will the requirements be excessive or particularly burdensome.

Or suppose your primary motivation for affiliating with a church is to find companionship in the search for meaning, in the quest to make sense of human existence. In that regard, you may find that the sermons take too much belief for granted and that none of the classes offered adults seem to be geared for wrestling with serious questions. Once again, an understanding of internal parish politics will often show you how to get what you want. Most churches have an individual or a committee in charge of adult education, or if they do not, they wish they did. The skeptic interested in dealing with ultimate concerns—the unanswerable questions— usually can get something established simply by volunteering to make the arrangements. Many times I have seen a relative newcomer organize a series of lectures and bring in people to lead discussions on subjects ranging from religion in American art to Christianity under communism. I have seen skeptics gather small groups to read and talk about books like *Zen and the Art of Motorcycle Maintenance* and *Until We Have Faces*. In nearly any Episcopal church you will find that at least two or three people will respond to an invitation from a fellow parishioner to discuss almost any subject. The person willing to take the initiative need never be wanting companions in the business of trying to make sense out of nonsense.

Investment in the Community

Perhaps a desire for companionship underlies all of the other longings that draw skeptics to church. A few years ago Bruce, a retired bachelor and former warden in our congregation, was dying of multiple myeloma. He wanted to die at home, but he had no family who could care for him except an elderly, crippled brother. When a member of the congregation heard about his request to spend his last days in familiar surroundings among people who cared about him, she organized volunteers so that every day fellow parishioners would be with him. Dozens of people wanted to be placed on the roster of visitors because they were aware of how much Bruce had contributed to the life of the church and the neighborhood. When I saw Bruce surrounded by companions in the last days of his life, I realized that even if I lost the last shred of my Christian convictions I would join a church and contribute whatever I could. I do not want to grow old and die alone. Bruce had companions at the end of his life because he had contributed in hundreds of little ways: he mowed the yard and trimmed the shrubs; he repaired the broken handle on the parish hall door; he greeted visitors on Sunday morning and he ushered at funerals; but most important, he was always there when someone needed him. As a consequence the church was there when he needed the rest of us. I do not mean to suggest the Bruce was calculating about all of this, but I stand by my observation. Although people who invest themselves in the life of a community receive no guarantees, they are much more likely to have companions when they need them than people who try to be independent and to remain aloof from mundane concerns.

One investment in a community that skeptics sometimes overlook is financial. I recall a conversation I once had with a skeptic who was offended by being asked to make a pledge of financial support for the church. He said he had given up on churches in his youth because they were always asking for money. When I asked him who was supposed to pay my salary and to pay for the heat and light, he replied, "The church."

Somehow he had developed the notion that churches had money. A few do have large endowments that produce enough income to pay all the bills, but the vast majority of Episcopal churches rely almost entirely on what the members choose to contribute.

Skeptics who have never contributed to the support of a church are often shocked to discover how much it costs to produce what they want. If they decide to take their financial responsibility seriously, however, they may still be at a loss to know how much is their fair share. The official standard in the Episcopal church is ten percent of current income, but in practice most of the responsible people only give half of this "tithe", as ten percent is called in the Bible, to the church, and give the other half to charity. People whose minds boggle at the prospect of giving away a tenth of their income may of course pick some other percentage, but in deciding how much to contribute, they should keep in mind a few of the mysterious truths about money: The cost of necessities nearly always rises faster than income. Nobody has enough money. Everyone can live on less money, and usually has done so. Money, like love, is a form of spiritual energy; people who contribute to the prosperity of others find prosperity.

The other thing you should keep in mind when considering the amount of a financial pledge is that "there are no secrets in parish life." A parish may have sealed pledges that only the treasurer sees. A parish may even have a system in which pledges are not signed—only the pledger and God know the amount pledged. But when the pledger makes a request for help, the community somehow has a sense if this person has made a responsible investment in their common life. Although most church leaders, including clergy, try their best to respond in an even-handed manner to all legitimate requests, their enthusiasm for helping will probably be influenced by the commitment demonstrated by the person asking for help.

Two observations attributed to Jesus in the Gospel according to St. Matthew aptly summarize what I have been trying to say: "Where your treasure is, there will your heart be also" and (6:21) "The measure you give will be the measure you get" (7:2).

Turning the Cheek and Talking Straight

Teachings attributed to Jesus by Matthew will also do well for the final point on internal parish politics. Most people can recite "if any one strikes you on the right cheek, turn to him the other also." Not so many, however, realize that turning the other cheek is just one side of a paradox in the teaching of Jesus. The other side is recorded in Matthew 18:15-20.

> If your brother sins against you, go and tell him his fault, between you and him alone. If he listens to you, you have gained your brother. But if he does not listen, take one or two others along with you, that every word may be confirmed by the evidence of two or three witnesses. If he refuses to listen to them, tell it to the church; and if he refuses to listen even to the church, let him be to you as a Gentile and a tax collector.

Jesus apparently thought that straight talk was as important as refusing to be vindictive. Both concepts are essential for skeptical people trying to get what they want from parish life. Trying to get even every time you get hurt is self-defeating, but so is pretending that nothing has gone wrong. In order to work the parish political system to personal advantage, a skeptical person must learn to behave within the constraints of this paradox. A willingness to forgive as well as a willingness to confront will open up possibilities with many members of a congregation, including the paid staff, but staff people are a special case.

The Care and Feeding of the Church Staff

The paid staff at a church may consist of any number, from just one part-time priest to an elaborate configuration of rector, assisting clergy, counselors, musicians, secretaries, book-keepers, sextons, and directors of programs for special groups such as the youth, the elderly, and the disadvantaged. Whether the staff is large or small, however, the skeptical person who wants something from the church will be well advised to follow the same general principle: take care of these people and they will take care of you.

An interest in improving the music can illustrate the importance of being considerate of the paid staff for getting what you want from a church. While maneuvering into a position of influence within the parish organization, the music lover will also be working on another level: winning the confidence of the person in charge of the music. Technically, the person in charge of the music will be the rector, vicar, or dean but in fact the person in the key position will usually be a director of music or an organist. Unfortunately, people who are extremely sensitive to church music are often insensitive to church musicians. They forget that musicians are not only beset by all the anxieties suffered by other human beings but are also made vulnerable by an artistic temperament. In short, they are easily bruised, and they tend to react to hurt by displays of temper or depression. Like other mortals, however, musicians often respond positively to well-deserved praise and to genuine concern. Over a period of time a few kind words, notes of appreciation, an occasional invitation to lunch, and a willingness to listen to the musician's description of the situation will not only get the music lover a fair hearing but will also assure the music lover of the information necessary for making constructive suggestions. Such an approach is pragmatically sound. It also happens to be the loving way to behave.

The people who work in the church office are worthy of special consideration. Some church members treat the secretaries and bookkeepers as if they were their private slaves, always ready to do their personal bidding and never needing to hear any mention of appreciation. I have seen people barge into the office and drop a sheaf of papers on the desk of the church secretary with an abrupt comment such as, "I need eighty copies of each of these for tonight's canvass meeting." Apparently it did not matter that at the time the secretary was on the telephone with a parishioner whose mother had just died, or that she was in the middle of producing the Sunday bulletin, or that she had told the abrupt gentleman to call her early in the week if he needed help with the canvass so she could work his requests into her schedule, or that he had not thanked her for the last time she had rescued him by working overtime to produce materials for his meeting. This kind of behavior will soon produce predictable results: no more help from the church office, or worse, the loss of a good staff person.

It really does not take much effort to get what you want from most office staff people. Treat them as if they were human beings and not part of the equipment. Excuse yourself for interrupting. Ask when they might have time to handle your request. If you have an emergency, explain the nature of your problem. Always thank them, and praise them for good work. In short, treat them as you would want to be treated if your positions were reversed and you will probably have no difficulty in getting any reasonable request satisfied.

Clergy are also staff people, but their position as spiritual leaders in the congregation puts them in a slightly different position from the rest of the paid staff. Some church members emphasize the difference to such an extent that they make the clergy ill at ease. In their dealings with the clergy, skeptical people are often in a better position to get what they want than are the believers in the congregation. Many Episcopal clergy prefer the company of skeptics because they enjoy the challenge of probing questions. Clergy tire very quickly in the presence of forced piety, but are stimulated by intellectually honest conversation. Skeptics who may want something from the clergy can build on this advantage if they will not only follow the principles already enumerated, but also pay attention to these suggestions:

1. Be specific in your expressions of appreciation. Never say, "I enjoyed your sermon", but instead mention a specific point, such as, "What you said in your sermon about doubt providing the energy necessary for faith makes a lot of sense, but I had never thought about doubt in those terms." 2. Be specific in your complaints, and deliver them in a sensitive manner. Say at what point you became lost in the sermon, or precisely what was done at your friend's funeral that upset you, but do so at a time and a place when you can show your concern and when clergy will have the best opportunity to respond with a minimum of defensiveness. 3. Be sure that you are complaining to the right person before you start. Many people make the mistake of complaining to the clergy about the failures of their fellow parishioners, such as the junior

warden who hasn't mowed the lawn or the treasurer who hasn't sent out the pledge statements. 4. Get to know the clergy. Take them out to lunch. The evenings not committed to parish business are often precious family times, but the middle of the day is usually a good time for conversation in a relaxed setting. 5. Publicly support positions taken by the clergy whenever you can do so in good conscience. Your objections on those occasions when you disagree will then have much more credibility. 6. Do what you can to make sure the parish treats the clergy responsibly: pays more than the absolute minimum, provides for continuing education time and funds, gives direct criticism while making sure that no negative judgments are being passed around behind the backs of the clergy and that positive assessments become public knowledge.

Perhaps the attention paid here to the needs of the clergy seems excessive, but the hard fact of parish life is that little can happen without clergy cooperation and support. Any skeptic who wants to get something that does not seem to be immediately available in the church will be more likely to succeed by working with the clergy than trying to work around them.

You may be looking for a church because you want to get married, or to have a baby baptized, or to bury one of your parents, or simply to find a place where you can ask questions for which there are no easy answers. If you have been put off in your search because you are skeptical of many religious propositions, I hope this book has been of help by showing you how you can preserve your intellectual integrity and still participate in the life of a church. You can legitimately set aside the interpretations that "believers" have imposed on the Christian heritage and find reflections of your fears and longings in the lore of the church. These reflections, which will appear as you participate in the rituals of the church, can help you understand your life and live your life more effectively.